Solving the world's problems

Solving the world's problems

give greed a chance

Ronnie Horesh

iUniverse, Inc.
New York Lincoln Shanghai

Solving the world's problems
give greed a chance

iUniverse books may be ordered through booksellers or by contacting:

iUniverse
2021 Pine Lake Road, Suite 100
Lincoln, NE 68512
www.iuniverse.com
1-800-Authors (1-800-288-4677)

ISBN: 0-595-33961-1

Printed in the United States of America

Contents

Introduction

This book is an attempt to bridge the gap between our potential as human beings and the reality. Our world has immense wealth in resources, technology, expertise and goodwill. In important ways, we have been remarkably successful. A very large number of us have a standard of living far higher than even the most privileged members of societies throughout almost all of human history. Yet we are very probably on the brink of global catastrophe of our own making. Climate change could wreak havoc with our natural environment. It could permanently damage entire ecosystems. It could cause rising sea levels and the spread of tropical diseases, either of which could imperil millions. There is no need to speculate about the other major threat to all of us: violent political conflict. Many millions have already died in the insanity of war, civil war and terrorism. Others live lives that are blighted by war or the fear of war. With the proliferation of weapons of mass destruction, violent political conflict now looms large over the entire world population.

No less disastrous to people in the poor countries are hunger, poverty and disease. And even in the developed countries—the richest societies in human history—social problems persist. There remain pockets of poverty and hopelessness and even among the materially better off there are many whose lives are blighted by crime.

The first part of this book will look at, and try to explain, the failures of current policymaking. It will try to find out why policymakers fail to solve social and environmental problems, despite our immense physical and intellectual resource endowment and near-universal consensus that the human race should survive and that our children should all have the opportunity to live lives as free as possible from poverty, hunger and despair. It will conclude first: that targeted outcomes should drive social and environmental policy; activities and

1

institutions should be entirely subordinated to the outcomes that we want to achieve, and these outcomes should be meaningful to natural persons, rather than corporate bodies. Second, market forces should be channelled into the achievement of these outcomes.

The rest of this book will suggest how we can re-orientate policymaking along those lines. The problem is how to inject market incentives into the achievement of targeted, meaningful, social and environmental goals. The solution offered—really more of a 'meta-solution'—is a new financial instrument, Social Policy Bonds.

Our arguments have ramifications for all existing policy institutions, because it is not only national governments, but also international bodies such as the United Nations and World Bank, and non-governmental organisations (NGOs), whose policies are collectively failing us. This book will suggest how they, and other concerned individuals, can use Social Policy Bonds to channel resources into helping solve social and environmental problems.

Our hope is that the issuing of Social Policy Bonds will lead to the creation of new institutions whose sole objective will be to achieve targeted social and environmental goals. The bonds may also lead to the reform of existing bodies that have lost their way over time. But the thrust of this book is not about the identity, structure or activities of institutions. Nor is this book overly preoccupied by the *size* of policymaking bodies whether they be international, national or local in character. This book's over-riding concern is that policy should be formulated in terms of outcomes that are meaningful to natural persons, and that people should have incentives to achieve these outcomes.

1

Policymaking today

The most obvious evidence that policymaking today is flawed is the persistence of severe social and environmental problems, despite humankind's immense scientific resources, its material wealth, and the goodwill and profound intellects of large numbers of well-meaning professionals and volunteers. In many rich and newly industrialised countries there have been remarkable increases in the material standard of living, but even here there are persistent and, in many cases, worsening social and environmental problems. Crime is generally rising, and there are pockets of deep poverty in most countries. Large, and increasing expenditure on public sector education still leaves some people behind; so much so that in the United Kingdom, for example, several million people lack basic literacy and numeracy skills.[1] More anecdotal evidence describes worsening mental health in the industrialised world.[2] And while the rich are significantly happier than the poor within any country at any moment, average happiness levels change very little as people's incomes rise in tandem over time.[3][4] All this despite government expenditures running at something like 40 per cent of the income[5] of the wealthiest societies in history, plus the efforts and resources of countless other non-governmental bodies, and private sector employees and volunteers.

In the developing countries many millions throughout the world suffer directly and indirectly from violent political conflict. They have to endure war, civil war, poverty, and diseases for which there are cures and treatments that are often effective and cheap.

3

People in all countries also face the real, but less quantifiable, threat of catastrophe arising from global social and environmental stresses. Of these, two in particular stand out. Violent political conflict carries with it the threats inherent in the proliferation of weapons of mass destruction. At the same time, whole populations and the entire global environment face disruption and potential disaster from the effects of climate change.

Why, despite numerous governments and other organisations ostensibly striving to solve our social and environmental problems, do they persist? Why is there such a gap between what can be achieved, and what is actually achieved and why is this gap arguably growing wider? Is it because we lack resources? Or is it because there is no real consensus over policy objectives?

Squandering resources: perverse subsidies

With military spending of $956 billion per annum, and rising,[6] it's not too difficult to point to resources that if redirected could alleviate the poverty of millions, especially in the developing countries. Such redirection will be called hopelessly idealistic, but there are less fey ways in which the rich world's national governments could, if they were minded, go about solving some of their own social and environmental problems. For proof that instead they squander resources we have only to look at perverse subsidies.

Perverse subsidies are those that are economically inefficient *and* socially inequitable *and* environmentally destructive. Almost all the developed countries' agricultural subsidies fall into this category. Support to producers in the developed countries as measured by the Organisation for Economic Cooperation and Development (OECD) amounted to $318 billion in the year 2002.[7] Most assistance continues to be given in the form of market price support and output payments. These forms of support insulate farmers from world markets and impose a burden on domestic consumers. They also badly distort production and trade, harming especially farmers in developing countries, and intensifying pressure on the environment. As well, being strongly correlated with output levels, they go mostly to the largest farmers. In the US, for instance, about 88 per cent of support goes to the largest (in terms of gross sales) 25 per cent of the farmers.[8] And the higher food prices that result from these policies bear most heavily on low-income consumers, for whom food constitutes a larger share of total household expenditure. Apart from large farmers, many of whom are very wealthy by any standards, the main beneficiaries of the panoply of agricultural support policies in the developed countries are the agribusiness industry and programme administrators,[9] while fraudsters also gain substantially.[10]

Agriculture is the best-documented perversely subsidised sector but there are others. Subsidies to private road transport include the hidden costs of providing road users with roads, space and complementary traffic services such as highway patrols, traffic management, and paramedics. For the years 1991 and 1989, two different studies estimated the net subsidies to road transport in the US at $55 billion and $174 billion, respectively, or 1 and 3 per cent respectively of that country's GDP.[11] (The wide range reflects the different estimates for parking subsidies and for providing complementary traffic services.) Questionable on many other grounds, road funding—as well as funding for public transport schemes—would appear to be an example of middle-class welfare. Most of the benefits of these works go overwhelmingly to those who have more money to spend on travel, and more time in which to do so.[12] The other major beneficiaries of government-funded infrastructure projects are construction companies worldwide: well-known as recipients of corporate welfare and very often criminally corrupt.[13]

The energy sector is also heavily subsidised. In the mid 1990s it was estimated that annual subsidies for energy in OECD countries were running at between $70 billion and $80 billion; their main purpose being to support energy production. Coal receives most subsidies, followed by nuclear energy and oil.[14]

More nebulous, but no less real, are the subsidies that the rich countries lavish on their armaments industries: a recent, well-researched, British study estimates that the subsidies provided to UK companies involved in defence exports are worth at least £453 million annually, and possibly up to £936 million.[14.5]

Estimates are bound to be imprecise, but it would be reasonable to put the total sums wasted on perverse subsidies in the developed countries at about 3 per cent of their combined GDP—this is equivalent to about 8 per cent of their governments' total spending. Governments in the developing countries are not much better: putting aside their lavish military spending they also subsidise energy, water use, road transport, water use and agriculture. What is especially striking about perverse subsidies, apart from their wastefulness and the damage they do, is their persistence in the face of evidence about their destructive role that stretches back for decades. Something is clearly very wrong with government's faculties of adaptation and response.

Perverse subsidies are essentially expensive ways of protecting sectoral investments and employment. They constitute sufficient evidence that governments mis-allocate significant resources. But they are only the most spectacular wastes of government funds, representing entire policies almost all of whose effects on society and the environment are negative. Other government failings are not always so obvious or quantifiable. Sometimes only certain elements of a programme are questionable, or only fractions of public funds may be misdirected or abused. Or government may be carrying out worthwhile activities inefficiently, so that their costs to the taxpayer are higher than necessary. One consequence is a certain fatalism about where our societies are heading and more specifically about what government can do about it. If this sounds far-fetched, we need only to look at the international community's delayed, muted responses to humanitarian crises or its efforts to relieve the causes of violent political conflict in Africa.

To summarise, we find that in many of the wealthiest societies that have ever existed in human history, there are significant pockets of deprivation, crime rates are high and rising, health services are plagued by too much demand and occasional scares, and public education seems always to be in crisis. Environmental problems are a growing cause for concern at all levels: local, national and global. Indeed the entire human population is now threatened by global environmental catastrophe and by the proliferation of weapons of mass destruction. These problems persist despite high levels of government spending and the less well-funded but laudable efforts of many non-governmental organisations. They cannot be attributed to insufficient resources.

The role of ideology

Perhaps the answer is that there is no agreement amongst policymakers over what are desirable goals for our societies, so they persist because we are pulling in different directions.

More than a decade ago, Francis Fukuyama, a State Department official, contended in his controversial essay (and later book) *The End of History*[15] that "the ineluctable spread of consumerist Western culture" presages "not just the end of the Cold War, or the passing of a particular period of postwar history, but the end of history as such: that is, the end point of mankind's ideological evolution." What is remarkable about this claim is that it is demonstrably true. For better or for worse, democratic capitalism and the mixed economies that characterise the developed countries are becoming world culture. There are now few serious ideological differences within the rich countries that have in the past led to violent conflict and that could explain their current failures. Few policymakers now say openly that their role is not to maximise social welfare for all their citizens. The ends of economic policy between political parties are broadly similar, not only in the rich world but in most developing countries also. There *are* differences, including ideological differences, over the presumed *ways* in which a society's social objectives will be achieved. But most of these differences are minor and have more to do with who carries out or benefits from particular programmes than with the broad thrust of policy.

The similarities are more compelling and more fundamental: all governments and almost all people want to support the deserving poor; all emphatically want to avoid global catastrophe, however caused. Few oppose the preservation of law and order, and few believe in violence as a policy of choice. We all want good basic health and education outcomes. Of course, what people say and what they truly want are different things, and political parties do have different perspectives on economic development. But is nevertheless striking how similar are the ostensible goals of governments and policymakers around the world.

Many of our social and environmental problems are too complex fully to understand. Violent political conflict and climate change, which we shall look at in detail below, can have a multitude of causes. Even the specialists often disagree, and not only on marginal matters. In some cases they will inevitably select the evidence that suits their predisposition. There are so many relationships, so many variables, and such large distances of time and space between cause and effect that, to disinterested non-specialists, there are very strong cases to be made on opposing sides of arguments about, for example, the Kyoto Protocol or conflict in the Middle East.

Rather than wait till Kyoto's scientific arguments are resolved—which could take many decades, or to pursue some abstract, contentious notion of justice in matters of human conflict, we might do better on efficiency grounds, to subordinate all our activities to our intended outcomes: climate stability, for example, or conflict reduction.

Anything but outcomes

Unfortunately governments and other policymaking bodies are adept at obscuring the relationship between people's stated goals and actual policy outcomes. They do so by expressing their policies in terms of just about everything—except actual policy outcomes.

Very often we hear politicians trying to defuse criticism of public sector schools, or hospitals, or whatever, by pointing to an increase in the budget for these organisations, as if increased spending will automatically lead to improved outcomes. They cannot imagine that favourable outcomes can be achieved other than by continuing to do existing activities more intensively, whether by increasing funding for existing organisations or by creating new organisations in the same image. In effect, our policymakers sacrifice many worthwhile policy goals to the priorities of institutions. These differ, sometimes markedly, from those of natural persons.

There are pointers as to what are existing organisations' true priorities. We need only look at the spirited, and often ingenious, defence of perverse subsidies mounted with straight faces by the organisations that stand to lose most if they are withdrawn. Or we can read that about half of the funds allocated to humanitarian relief and development aid organisations stays with these bodies.[16]

Box: Essential terms

Inputs Expenditure, or those factors of production, such as staff, accommodation, other supplies, or other resources, that are used to produce goods and services. Amongst the inputs devoted to lowering crime, for example, would be: police numbers, numbers of patrol cars, and expenditure on policing.

Outputs Products that are directly attributable to the performance of an agency, such as number of reports produced and distributed or number of buildings constructed. Outputs of a crime-fighting agency could be: numbers of police on the beat or on patrol at a time, number of police stations open 24 hours a day, number of toll-free phone lines, and the proportion of police emergency phone calls answered within 15 seconds.

Outcomes, objectives, goals Desirable sets of circumstances that are likely to be influenced by an agent's outputs *and* by factors outside agents' control. An outcome that might be targeted by crime-fighting agencies is a crime rate 10 per cent lower than in the previous year (as measured by number of reported crimes, or responses to victim surveys). The terms 'objectives' and 'goals' are used synonymously in this text to mean desired outcomes.

Large sums of cash are obviously available to international organisations and national governments whose remit is to help solve social and environmental problems, but *they are not given in ways that encourage the achievement of outcomes that are meaningful to real people.*

We accept that private sector firms behave as profit maximisers, within the constraints set up by a legislative framework, their code of ethics and the unwritten rules that govern their behaviour. Our expectations of governments, as bodies explicitly charged with achieving social and environmental goals are different, and it is especially unfortunate when, as so many national governments do, they fail to fulfil their raison d'etre: to achieve social and environmental outcomes that are meaningful to their citizens.

It is even worse when they help to perpetuate a dysfunctional policymaking environment. This they do by influencing it in ways that ensure their continued survival. Those who are successful in attracting funding—the recipients of perverse subsidies and other forms of corporate welfare, for example—can use the resources so gained to entrench themselves more deeply in the policymaking process. It is a self-reinforcing process, which means that the already significant differences between actual policy outcomes and the desired outcomes of natural persons tends to widen over time. It will continue to widen until we re-orientate the way in which we formulate social and environmental policy.

Of course, not all our social and environmental ills are indictments of international bodies or national governments. There are plenty of natural disasters; there is quite possibly, an *overall* lack of resources, and there is a sufficiently large absolute number of people striving officiously to negate the goodwill of the people who work to improve global welfare. The task of Social Policy Bonds will be not to bring about utopia, but to ensure that a larger fraction of whatever resources are devoted to solving our world's social and environmental problems actually help achieve their goal.

A Social Policy Bond regime would:

- Decide on targeted environmental and social outcomes that are inextricably linked to the improved welfare of natural persons; and

- Inject the market's incentives and efficiencies into achieving these outcomes.

Social Policy Bonds will encourage the efficient allocation of society's scarce resources into the achievement of the outcomes that society wants to achieve. They seek to refocus our ingenuity on policy ends and to link—effectively and inextricably—financial incentives to the achievement of these ends.

2

Climate change and violent political conflict: current approaches

Introduction

In this chapter we focus on two global concerns: climate change and violent political conflict. Either could be disastrous for the human race, and both are, in this author's view, being addressed inadequatelyt. For these reasons they deserve our attention. We shall mention briefly, at the end of the chapter, other social problems.

Climate change

Climate change is probably our most urgent environmental challenge. The evidence that the global climate is changing is substantial and growing. That said, scientists are divided as to how fast climate is changing, the likely effects of climate change and how much we can do about it, while politicians and economists are divided about how much we *should* do about it. The uncertainties are huge—table 1 shows how radically forecasts can change over just a few years—but even slight changes in the climate could unleash disasters on an unimaginable scale. The most grievous impact will be on those least able to adapt: that is, the poor: large numbers of people in the developing countries are at immediate risk, either from rising sea levels or from more frequent adverse climatic events. So, despite legitimate questions about whether and how fast the climate is changing, it would be irresponsible to sit back and do nothing.

Table 1 *

Year of Forecast	Rate of Warming	Greenhouse Effect by 2030	
		Temperature Rise	Sea Level Rise
1988	0.8 C per decade	3.0 C	20 to 150 cm
1990	0.3 C per decade	1.2 C	15 to 40 cm
1995	0.2 C per decade	0.8 C	5 to 35 cm

* Warming forecasts taken from the 1988 'World Conference on the Changing Atmosphere: Implications for Global Security' held in Toronto, Canada in 1988, the 1990 First Assessment Report of the Intergovernmental Panel on Climate Change (IPCC) and the 1995 Second Assessment Report of the IPCC.
Source: Dr Brian O'Brien, October 1997.[17]

Current approach

The current approach to the climate change problem is to invest huge political and economic resources in the Kyoto Protocol. This seeks to limit what is thought to be the cause of climate change: emissions of greenhouse gases. The greenhouse gases are thought to trap heat, causing the earth's temperature to rise. The UN's Intergovernmental Panel on Climate Change (IPCC) estimates a range of warming between 1.4°C and 5.8°C over the next century. Each of the greenhouse gases is thought to have different effects on the climate. Kyoto translates these into carbon dioxide equivalents, using ratios fixed in the 1990s. It seeks to cap the emissions of the rich countries to just below their 1990 levels.

The Kyoto Protocol does not oblige developing countries to accept binding limits on their emissions in the near future so, even if all industrialised countries honour their commitments to reduce pollution, the quantity of greenhouse gases in the atmosphere will continue to grow. About 85 per cent of the world's nations, with about 75 per cent of the world's population, do not have to cut emissions under Kyoto—that includes China, which currently accounts for more than one eighth of world emissions. A model by one member of the IPCC indicates that Kyoto would reduce an expected temperature increase of 2.1°C in 2100 to an increase of 1.9°C instead. Or, to put it another way, Kyoto will postpone the temperature increase that the planet would have experienced in 2094 by just six years, to 2100.[18] Advocates for Kyoto see it as only a first step. But is it a step in the wrong direction?

What's wrong with Kyoto

Kyoto's objective is mis-specified. Its success or failure will be measured entirely by changes in quantities of anthropogenic emissions of greenhouse gases. This means that it will not strive to achieve a reduction in total green-house gas emissions. Nor will it aim for a change in the composition of the atmosphere. Still less will it aim to arrest climate change or mitigate its negative impacts. Kyoto's only goal is to reduce anthropogenic greenhouse gas emissions.

Kyoto suffers from the same flaw as many of our other environmental and social policies: it assumes that governments know the best ways of achieving our goals. But the biological and physical relationships involved in climate change are many and complex. Even specialists in climatology disagree about the degree to which the multitude of biological and physical variables cause climate change.

Kyoto will do little to encourage people to explore all these complex relationships. In particular, it will do little to encourage people to:

1. respond to new knowledge about the causes of climate change,
2. investigate new activities that could mitigate climate change more efficiently than reducing anthropogenic greenhouse gas emissions, and
3. respond to local effects and changing circumstances.

1 Causes of climate change

We know very little about the causes of climate change and the likely course it will take. How the climate responds to changes that might already be in train is critical: feedbacks may amplify or attenuate any initial warming. Nobody yet knows, for instance, whether climate change will affect clouds in ways that generate positive or negative feedbacks.[19] Our knowledge on such subjects may be scanty, but it can improve dramatically over time.

Even if we find that anthropogenic greenhouse gases contribute far more to climate change than originally thought, Kyoto can do little in response. As I write this, in August 2004, research is being published showing that 'solar dimming', the reduction in sunlight reaching the earth owing to the effects of clouds, air pollution and aerosols in the atmosphere, appears to have much greater effect than first imagined, [20] which means that the contribution of greenhouse gases to climate change may have been underestimated. Kyoto has no provision to impose even lower limits on greenhouse gases in response to such research conclusions, however necessary they might be.

It is also quite possible that climate stability will be greatly assisted—or worsened—by natural phenomena. There is potential for new scientific solutions and for natural phenomena to invalidate the Kyoto approach almost overnight. The effect of Kyoto then would be to continue to impose costs out of all proportion to any benefit. But *there is no provision for reducing these costs*, or for backing out of—or accelerating—Kyoto's obligations in the event our knowledge or circumstances change to the extent that Kyoto becomes extravagant or insignificant. The Kyoto approach ensures that the entire planet will continue to bear the cost of greenhouse gas cutbacks, regardless of whether these cutbacks are necessary to, or efficient in, achieving climate stability. Indeed it is not impossible that cutbacks of greenhouse gas emissions actually increase climate instability. But Kyoto does not allow for that possibility.

2 Investigating new activities

Kyoto prejudges how its goal is to be achieved. It embodies the assumption that reducing anthropogenic greenhouse gas emissions is the best way of mitigating climate change. But Kyoto's objective is so broad, and we know so little about the scientific and ecological relationships, that it would be better to encourage a wide range of potentially beneficial activities than to specify in advance, armed only with current scientific knowledge, how that objective shall be achieved. An ideal policy approach would not discourage research into, and application of, new, more efficient solutions than those that can currently be envisaged by policymakers. A policy such as Kyoto, which seeks to constrain certain pre-defined activities may not be optimally efficient because our knowledge of the results of these activities, and of ones yet to be discovered or investigated, is expanding rapidly.

Kyoto is not incompatible with stabilising the climate, but there is little evidence to suggest that it is the most efficient way of doing so. If cutting back greenhouse gas emissions really were the most efficient way of achieving climate stability, then that is what people should be encouraged to do. But they should come to that conclusion themselves, having tried out a wide range of alternative approaches, many of which could be more cost-effective in that they would do more to stabilise the climate, per dollar spent, than Kyoto. People should not be compelled to comply with a top-down approach that incorporates the very limited scientific knowledge that exists today. We need measures that encourage people to investigate new activities that may be more cost-effective at stabilising the climate, or mitigating the worst effects of climate change.

A large number of scientists, technologists, engineers and biologists, in countless research bodies the world over, are looking at the causes and effects of climate change and how to deal with or mitigate them. But there is no overall mechanism in place to allocate funding for these bodies on the basis of their likely cost-effectiveness. Within some countries, cost-effectiveness may be one criterion used to allocate funding. But in general, funding for a particular body depends on a range of factors, including ones that have little relevance to efficiency. These can include the body's existing size and level of funding, the number of people it employs, its contribution to the local economy, its historical record, its fundraising skills, its public image, the charisma of its senior staff and their relationship to important politicians or celebrities.

Each institution may well be—indeed, most probably, are—run by people with the highest integrity and scientific knowledge, and it is quite possible that *within each body*, funds will be allocated impartially and with a view to obtaining the best result for each dollar outlay. The problem is that there is no overall structure of incentives that will ensure that funds will be allocated *between* these bodies, or to the creation of new ones, according to their *overall* efficiency at maximising the cost-effectiveness at which we can reduce climate change.

One effect of Kyoto may be to starve promising projects of funds because they do nothing to reduce anthropogenic greenhouse gas emissions. It is unlikely, perhaps, but it is possible, that *increasing the planet's albedo*—its reflective-ness—by, for example, launching mirrors or reflective particles into orbit around the Earth orbiting, could reflect a significant proportion of incoming radiation back out again, and so play a large role in achieving climate stability. But such an initiative may well have a contribution to make, as one of a wide range of diverse projects, all aimed at achieving a stable climate. Kyoto, despite all its vast expenditure, will do nothing to investigate this possibility. With its sole target of reduced anthropogenic greenhouse gas emissions, Kyoto would leave projects that raise albedo out of the reckoning when disbursing funds.

Or take another example: the development of *genetically engineered cyanobac-teria* that can soak up atmospheric carbon dioxide and convert it into a raw material for biodegradable plastic. In the last few years scientists in Japan announced that they can make the cyanobacterium (*Synechococcus* sp.) produce up to 10 per cent of its dry weight as polyhydroxybutric acid (PHB). When PHB is joined in a copolymer with hydroxyvalerate it produces a biodegrad-able plastic. And the only raw materials that the altered bacteria need to pro-duce the PHB are water and carbon dioxide. The scientists wanted to use the engineered organism to extract carbon dioxide from exhaust gases in facto-ries—simultaneously reducing emissions of a greenhouse gas while making a useful product.[21]

Kyoto, of course, does not even target atmospheric composition, let alone cli-mate stability, so there are no global incentives to investigate cyanobacteria further. Again, cyanobacteria are unlikely to be the sole solution to the climate change problem. But the important point is that they and atmospheric mirrors are potential contributors to a solution to climate change that could collec-tively be far more efficient than the single-issue policy that Kyoto represents.

The political and financial resources involved in trying to achieve climate sta-bility via Kyoto are colossal, so its inefficiencies are going to consume signifi-cant resources that could otherwise be used to solve real social and environmental problems. Kyoto is going to conduct its climate-stabilising activities as if science stopped in the year 2000. There will be other projects aimed at finding other ways of mitigating climate change. But it is clear that their funding will not be allocated according to how successful or cost-effective these methods will be. The lion's share of funding will go into efforts aimed at reducing our greenhouse gas emissions. Actually, and to be more accurate and pessimistic, these efforts will be concentrated on complying with Kyoto—which is not the same thing at all. A likely scenario is that many greenhouse gas emitting processes will simply shift from countries that are bound by Kyoto to countries that are not. In any case exploitation of new initiatives will take a back seat. The consequences of this flaw could be disastrous.

3 Responding to local effects and changing circumstances

Kyoto fails to provide incentives to experiment with different activities in different regions. This matters because, while climate change is a global problem, many of its effects are local. It may be preferable to aim to eliminate or mitigate such local adverse events, rather than their assumed causes. As far as human welfare is concerned, it could be much more cost-efficient to build seawalls in some parts of the world, or to implement flood control programmes, than to reduce greenhouse gas emissions.

Kyoto will provide no means of reallocating resources either to those parts of the world most in need, or in response to changing events. All Kyoto's efforts will be focused on cutting back anthropogenic gas emissions, at its own pace, and regardless of the differing effects of climate change on different parts of the world.

The way forward

Achieving a stable climate will mean investigating a wide range of diverse approaches that don't have anything to do with greenhouse gas emissions—but Kyoto will do nothing to encourage such research. Reducing greenhouse gas emissions or sequestering carbon à la Kyoto might turn out to be helpful and cost-effective. But what if new science tells us either that greenhouse gases are not as important as originally thought, or that there are far more cost-effective ways of achieving climate stability? Kyoto would grind on, with its expensive and futile controls on greenhouse gas emissions. As its critics point out Kyoto's costs are large, upfront, and definite, while its benefits are small, remote and uncertain.

Our problem, of course, is *not* greenhouse gases; it is climate change. So our objective should not be to cut back on greenhouse gas emissions, but *to achieve climate stability*. A successful policy would encourage those who help stabilise the climate, *however they do so*.

Climate is extremely complex. What affects it, and the effects it has, cannot yet be determined with much precision. Our knowledge, however, is expanding all the time. Similarly, the scope for technology that mitigates the effects of climate change is improving constantly. What we need is a way of dealing with climate change that channels improving knowledge into the outcome that we seek. The best way of addressing climate change would not embody the assumption that it knows exactly how the Earth's climate is changing, what is causing it to change, and what is the best way of dealing with any change. It would not ignore a potentially catastrophic problem, but it would try to be as cost-effective as possible, because the human and financial costs of dealing with climate change are colossal. An ideal policy would stimulate the investigation and adoption of promising new technologies, and be responsive to our fast-increasing knowledge about the causes and effects of climate change. It would most probably seek to constrain the negative effects of climate change, especially in areas where doing so would maximise the benefits, however measured, per dollar expenditure. At the same time it would do little to discourage any positive effects of climate change. Ideally too, it would use markets, the best way yet devised of allocating society's scarce resources, to channel people's self-interest into achieving climate stability.[1]

If such a solution could be found, it would be certain to attract more support than Kyoto both from decision makers and ordinary people. Such support is essential, because stabilising the climate is going to entail enormous costs and sacrifices.

Ranking high up there with climate change as a complex and critical global concern is that of violent political conflict.

----

1. Kyoto does allow for the operation of markets in permits to emit greenhouse gases, but these would aim only to make Kyoto's greenhouse gas emission reduction agenda more efficient—not to allocate resources between different ways of addressing climate change.

Violent political conflict

The problem

In the 1990s 3.6 million people, most of them civilians, were killed in conflict.[22] In 2001 alone the United Nations was attempting to help an estimated 21.8 million refugees and internally displaced persons as the result of conflict.[23] Most victims of conflict, especially in recent times, are non-military. Since the end of the Cold War, 90 per cent of those killed in conflict have been non-combatants, compared with 15 per cent at the beginning of the 20th century[24] and 65 per cent in World War II, including holocaust victims.[25]

There are some encouraging trends. The end of the Cold War in 1990 has seen a sharp downward trend in such components of global warfare as ethnic rebellion,[26] in forcibly dislocated populations,[27] and in autocratic 'command' authority systems. The number and magnitude of armed conflicts within and between states have lessened since the early 1990s by nearly half.[28] These trends have been paralleled by the upward trend in democracy: democratic governments now outnumber autocratic governments two to one and continue to be more successful than autocracies in resolving violent societal conflicts.[29] [30] More conflicts are being settled;[31] in particular those over self-determination, when ethnic groups gain greater autonomy and power-sharing within existing states.[32]

But the world has not entered a new era of universal peace. Some researchers have reported a substantial increase in serious wars (i.e. wars with greater than 1000 battle-related deaths in a given year) in the latter 1990s. Others have made the even bolder claim that the general downward trend in armed conflict has been reversed in recent years.[33] New kinds of war are being fought that are less disciplined and more spontaneous than the old. It is in these 'low-intensity' wars, occurring in recent times in Ivory Coast, Somalia, Sudan, Liberia, East Timor and the former Yugoslavia, that the civilian proportion of the dead reaches 90 per cent.[34]

Meanwhile the *potential* for catastrophe, represented by the proliferation of weapons of mass destruction, especially nuclear, is increasing. The total world nuclear stockpile now consists of over 36 800 warheads. (In addition to deployed nuclear warheads, thousands more are held in reserve and are not counted in official declarations.[35]) Countries as poor as North Korea now have the capacity to threaten neighbouring countries with nuclear weapons. One expert estimates that, barring radical new antiproliferation steps, the odds of a terrorist nuclear attack occurring in the ten years from 2004 are about even.[36]

Root causes and conflict prevention

If the relationship between anthropogenic greenhouse gas emissions and climate change seems too shaky a base for our policymakers' entire climate change mitigation strategy, what about conflict prevention? Are there are any reliable relationships that would be amenable to a top-down approach? Are there precursors to conflict that an international body could work on, with the aim of preventing conflict? We look first at the 'root causes' issue, than at the way institutions have approached it.

Root causes

To those of us fortunate to be distant spectators of violent political conflict it all seems very simple. War between country A and country B is inevitable, we think, because they both want the same piece of land. Or the inhabitants of country A believe in X while the inhabitants of country B believe in Y. Or within country C the ruling party are of ethnic group D and rich, while the masses are of ethnic group E and poor. Once conflict is actually happening, it is not difficult for outsiders to give plausible reasons for its occurrence, or even its inevitability.

Poverty, ignorance, despair, and differences of wealth, ethnicity, religion,[37] class, culture or ideology: all these are thought to be some of the 'root causes' of war and violence. So are inequalities in access to resources, scarcity and economic decline, insecurity, the violation of human rights, exclusion or persecution of sectoral groups, and state failures including declining institutional and political legitimacy and capacity. Other key foundations for conflict could be historical legacies, regional threats, the availability of weapons, economic shocks, and the extension or withdrawal of external support.[38] Demography is also significant: large numbers of unemployed males can catalyse conflict.

Sometimes inward factors are cited; such as individual pathologies; perhaps a history of being abused that predisposes someone to take up violence in later life. Often blamed too are the media, and the frequency with which our children are exposed to images of violence—especially when violence is presented as an acceptable and effective way of solving problems.

No doubt all these factors can and do play a part in fomenting and fanning the flames of conflict. But even aside from the impossibility of eliminating every potential cause of conflict, there is no *inevitability* that these causes will lead to war. Selective memory has strengthened these linkages in the collective mind, but for each of these 'root causes' there are examples that disprove any simple cause-and-effect relationship. There are dozens of countries in which people of different ethnicity and religion live happily side-by-side. There are also thousands of decent, peaceable and fulfilled adults who as children were horribly abused. One researcher into child abuse concluded that it does increase the risk of later criminality—but not always. The 'intergenerational transmission of violence is not inevitable,' she wrote.[39] There are many instances of land disputes that have ended. Take, for example, the border between Scotland and England, once the setting of a 300-year old series of bloody conflicts, now as peaceful as any border in the world. The Swiss have a high rate of gun ownership and an enviable absence of internal political conflict, as well as a low rate of gun crime. Japan is still a relatively peaceful society, but one in which lurid depictions of violence are avidly produced, promulgated and consumed, and have been for many years. Paul Collier and the World Bank, examining the world's civil wars since 1960, concluded that although tribalism is often a factor it is rarely the main one. They also found that societies composed of several different ethnic and religious groups were actually *less* likely to experience civil war than homogeneous societies.[40]

It would seem likely, then, that political violence cannot be *inextricably* linked to one, or even several, root causes. What could be a root cause of conflict in one region can be irrelevant in another. Elimination of supposed root causes, such as poverty, could alleviate tension in one particular conflict, but it could conceivably by, say, allowing more to be spent on weapons, inflame conflict in another. Availability of small arms in most societies probably does provoke or aggravate—the low Swiss murder rate, for example, is underpinned by strict gun control laws. There is no formula connecting any alleged root cause with conflict in ways that can be meaningful in the sense that removing it will always and inevitably lessen the chance of conflict.

As well, the factors that generate conflict may differ from those that make it feasible. In general, the existence of some form of grievance, whether economic, political, or social in origin, appears to be the most persuasive motivation for conflict. Economic motivations—whether the pursuit of resources for war-financing or for elite self-enrichment—appear more significant in sustaining, prolonging, and transforming conflict. The role of valuable natural resources is more ambivalent. They can make conflict more feasible when grievances already exist, as they offer a ready means of financing rebellion. But they can also become a source of grievance in themselves, if state institutions responsible for their management instead engage in corruption.[41] It is not always clear in which way is the direction of causation. In some cases, resource competition can exacerbate civil war. In others, civil war can exacerbate competition over resources.

Neither is it always clear which particular 'root causes' are operating even once a conflict has started. Explanations for the civil war in Lebanon from 1975–90 centred on ethnic or ideological causes of the conflict. But since the end of the conflict, economic developments, and rampant corruption in particular, seem to imply that economic opportunities were probably more important. The civil war resulted in the entry of new actors and an unprecedented rise in the level of social and political power, financial accumulation, and exercise of violence surrounding pre-existing, illegal drug-related activities. For local militias, drugs not only provided a means by which to pay wages, procure arms, and materiel, but also a source of capital accumulation among their leaders and middlemen. This trade resulted in trans-communal, regional cooperation between producers and militias, who negotiated the division of labour and took a share of the profits. These groups, therefore, had a collective interest in prolonging the war. The authorities have since done little to dismantle the drug networks and their factories. As a result, there has been long-term integration of these networks into the international drug market. Satisfaction of 'greed' in the name of 'creed' would have been impossible if not for cooperation across allegedly 'intractable' communal boundaries.[42]

These findings echo the pioneering work of Lewis Fry Richardson, who gathered data on all the wars of recent times, that is from 1820 to 1949. Rather than ranking wars by historical importance, or by relevance to later events, he picked the most objective measure he could find: the number killed, and focussed on those conflicts that killed more than 3000, for which the data were reasonably complete. There were 108 such conflicts during the 130-year period of study described in his seminal *Statistics of Deadly Quarrels*.[43] World Wars I and II together accounted for some 36 million deaths, or about 60 percent of all the deaths of his study period. (This total excludes those caused by famine and disease associated with war.[44]) While compiling his list of wars, Richardson noted the various items that historians mentioned as possible irritants or pacifying influences, and then he looked for correlations between these factors and belligerence. The results were almost uniformly disappointing. There were tendencies or correlations, but no unambiguous causal relationships. So states tended to become involved in wars in proportion to the number of states with which they have common frontiers, though in proportion to their possible contacts for war-making, sea powers seem to have been less belligerent than land powers. Richardson's own suppositions about the importance of arms races were not confirmed; he found evidence of a preparatory arms race in only 13 out of 315 cases. Richardson was a proponent of Esperanto, but found that similarity and difference of language appeared to have little influence on the occurrence of wars, contrary to the belief of some advocates of universal languages. Economic indicators were equally unhelpful: economic causes seem to have featured directly in fewer than 29 per cent of the wars since between 1820 and 1949. The statistics neither confirm nor refute the ideas that war is mainly a struggle between the rich and the poor or that commerce between nations creates bonds that prevent war.[45]

So it is not always obvious, even after a long conflict has ended, what its 'root causes' were, and perhaps the very notion of a 'root cause' needs questioning. It implies that factors such as 'poverty' or 'ethnicity' can be removed from their social context and somehow dealt with, and that then peace will follow. But human societies are complex. Poverty can feed grievance, but grievance can be a result of poverty.

An important conclusion then is that no single formula, no single set of parameters will always lead to conflict, or guarantee freedom from conflict. Indeed, even the notion of 'causation' in this context is questionable. Perhaps we should leave the last word to Tolstoy:

> The deeper we delve in search of these causes the more of them we discover, and each single cause or series of causes appears to us equally valid in

itself, and equally false by its insignificance compared to the magnitude of the event.[46]

Conflict prevention

What happens when today's institutions try to deal with the supposed root causes of conflict? There has recently been a laudable shift of conflict-resolution resources away from containing, mitigating and terminating active conflicts and toward preventing conflict.[47] Conflict prevention aims to deter conflicts and crises before they escalate: it comes into play early in a conflict and addresses what are thought to be the conflict's causes, building early warning and other institutional capacities to anticipate and cope with conflicts early on. These new methods to anticipate and keep incipient conflicts from erupting have joined older techniques of managing and resolving existing conflicts.[48] They are the way in which our current institutions try to discover, and defuse, the root causes of conflict. How are they performing?

The United Nations been criticised for institutional weakness and inflexibility in its approach to preventing conflict. There is no single UN agency responsible for conflict prevention. The Secretary-General has designated the Department of Political Affairs the focal point for conflict prevention initiatives, but numerous other departments, funds, and agencies are also engaged in preventive work. Coordination and mainstreaming of prevention is thus important. Recent reforms have helped raise the profile of prevention and improved the quality and effective transmission of relevant data and analysis throughout the UN system. But it is accepted that, since prevention can often seem to be everyone's business, it may, at times, seem to fall at no one's door.[49]

Perhaps the single official whose mandate is solely conflict prevention is the Organization for Security and Co-operation in Europe's High Commissioner on National Minorities, and his charge allows him to act only in pre-crisis situations; if they heat up, he must disengage. Another example: the UN High Commissioner for Refugees can only alleviate refugees' plight, not address the forces that caused it. More fundamental criticisms concern the structure of the UN Security Council, set up 50 years ago, in a world in which there were several powers in the top tier. To make the system workable all were given a veto. Today's world has but one such power, the United States, and the old structure is seen by some as inappropriate and dangerously irrelevant. And the

Security Council, though technically empowered to act on threats to international peace and security that arise within member countries, has mainly concerned itself with inter-state conflicts. Yet the 15 most deadly conflicts in, for example, 2001—those that killed over 100 people—were all intra-state conflicts, but all of them were directly affected by external actors and 11 of them spilled over international borders. Eleven of the conflicts have lasted for eight or more years.[50]

Many overseas aid programmes have, as an implicit objective, conflict prevention. But few donors exert the leverage that they could. In fact, development assistance can even, inadvertently, contribute to conflict. There are some difficult questions that need a flexible, pragmatic and most importantly, peace-orientated approach to answer. Mechanisms should evaluate the effects of aid on the probability of its increasing the likelihood of conflict. How benefits from aid projects are controlled and distributed might well aggravate conflict. Is western-style democracy likely to increase conflict? What about rapid economic development and globalisation? It might make economic sense to help finance a port, a road or a dam. But these facilities can enhance a national or local tyrant's position and make aggression more viable.

Why the current approach may be suboptimal

Government agencies and international organisations concerned with conflict are still mainly geared towards dealing with conflict once it has become violent, rather than preventing it arising in the first place. Too often in today's world the international community becomes involved in such conflict-prevention activities as mediation and peacekeeping only when the protagonists are facing each other or have actually begun armed conflict. There is also some institutional reluctance to become involved. Many development professionals, for example, see the more immediate causes of national conflicts as 'getting into politics' and thus something that should be left to military agencies,[51] or as interference in a country's internal affairs.

Many international agencies, especially those created during the Cold War, have discrete 'specific and defined sets of problems', and concern themselves with issues such as arms control, development, security assistance, health, or agriculture. Their distinct functions often mean that these agencies work in isolation from each other and sometimes at cross-purposes. One agency may be trying to prevent violent conflicts, while another (or another part of the same agency) may be doing things that aggravate them. There have been recent examples of aid being used to fuel conflict, or of the intent of trade sanctions being subverted, so that a repressive regime is the main beneficiary.[52]

Research suggests that conflict could be mitigated by diverting foreign aid in an armed conflict area to those countries contiguous to a civil war, especially those with longer common borders, since these are most prone to civil-war spillovers.[53] Governments could authorise or refuse arms exports applications by reference to factors such as the occurrence of armed conflicts, a state's human rights record and its level of militarization.[54] There is a strong case too, for trying innovative policies, some of which cannot effectively be performed by government, or government-funded agencies. These could include subsidising of anti-hate broadcasts, or trust-building measures which, because of their very nature, are viewed with suspicion when undertaken by officially approved bodies.

In all these areas, there should be incentives for organisations and their staff to act preventively, which may mean going beyond traditional job descriptions. Aid organisations, such as international or domestic NGOs monitoring human rights, and others should be encouraged to monitor countries' domestic behaviour and to alert the world community to possible violent conflicts, repression or dispersion of nuclear technology.

The approaches of the United Nations and its subsidiary bodies appear to be rife with the same deficiencies as those of their contributing governments. They are centralised, unexposed to competition and, in almost all most cases, not subject to the disciplines of effective self-evaluation. In many instances, their activities are also uncoordinated with those of NGOs, whose own spending is probably more flexible and efficient.

Take as one example, the appalling Rwandan genocide, which highlighted the dependence of this centralised decision-making on the whims of the UN membership. In 1994 the UN was begging for troops to send to Rwanda after the genocide started, but the African states refused. By the time troops finally did go in to Rwanda, much of the genocide had already taken place.

Former officers of the now defunct private military company, Executive Outcomes, provided documentation showing how they could have had troops on the ground in Rwanda within two weeks of being called. 'For $150 million they could have ended the genocide—imagine how many hundreds of thousands of innocent African lives could have been saved. There is no imaginable way that the UN could do such a task so quickly and so cheaply.'[55] That is merely one, tragic, example of how the effectiveness of the UN was held back by the politics and infighting of its members. Anecdotal evidence of this kind does not prove that market forces are always superior to public sector approaches. But it does suggest that those charged with conflict-reduction should be able to use markets when doing so would be more efficient.[56] In that way, the efficiencies and incentives of the market could be injected into the achievement of the social goal of conflict reduction.

After all, these incentives operate all too freely in the market for the weaponry that creates so much mayhem and misery. So much so that world military expenditure in 2003 was estimated at $956 billion.[57] Global spending on arm procurement accounts for between 20–30 per cent of military spending, the bulk of which goes to operations, maintenance and personnel.[58] By contrast, extraordinarily few global resources are committed to the prevention, management, or resolution of the world's most prevalent wars, almost all of which take place in poor countries. Nor, in relative terms, is much spent on peacekeeping and post-conflict reconstruction. The annual budget for UN peacekeeping was about $2.60 billion in 2002 and is estimated at about $2.63 billion for the year to 30 June 2003.[59] Preventive diplomacy missions cost only a tiny fraction of this amount.[60]

Of interest too is that many of the late 1990s' most serious wars involved conflicts over the control of black market commodities and assets that can be easily liquidated through illicit trade, such as drugs and diamonds. In contrast to conflict-reduction, the global arms trade has become increasingly privatised,[61] and so is most probably realising the benefits that come from pluralism—in sad contrast to conflict-reduction agencies.

Public choice theory would have it that international peacekeeping organisations are inherently cynical, in the sense that their overriding interest is to perpetuate their own existence. The truth is, we do not know whether these organisations are effective, ineffective, or even counter-effective in minimising conflict. Still less do we know whether they are efficient, in terms of achieving a worthwhile reduction in conflict per unit dollar outlay. Most probably, their performance varies markedly, though it is likely their existence as fora within which people from different countries interact, however ineffectually, serves a positive purpose, most of the time. Many of these organisations suffer from is lack of resources—at least in comparison with those who profit from conflict. Unfortunately there is no definitive way of showing that more funding would bring about more peace, or that such funding would be the most cost-effective way of reducing conflict.

In short, there are no mechanisms in place to evaluate, in an over-arching way, the distribution of conflict-reduction resources to make sure that they are achieving the best possible return for their outlay and nor are there incentives to set up such evaluation systems. The widespread presence of violent political conflict, the human cost of conflict, and the potential for further conflict; all suggest that it is worth investigating new approaches, even in the absence of definitive proof that anything new will work.

A second and related problem though is that neither the organisations whose remit is conflict reduction, nor the people that work for them, are paid according to results. They have only indirect incentives to seek out and develop those ways of minimising conflict that are most cost-effective. They might even face subtle disincentives to achieve their supposed objectives. This is not to say that employees are especially lazy or incompetent. They behave rationally given the financial and nonfinancial incentives on offer, but these incentives do not consistently reward the achievement of desired outcomes. There is no question that the people who work for these organisations are competent, hard-working and well-meaning. But however well-intentioned, neither these bodies nor their agents are rewarded in ways that are linked to their success in achieving peaceful resolution of political conflict.

Let us be clear what we are saying here. The individuals who work for these organisations are no doubt highly motivated and derive immense personal satisfaction from seeing their work translated into a reduced level of worldwide political conflict. No: lack of pecuniary incentives has two other dimensions. First, the funding of these bodies bears no relationship to their success or otherwise in reducing conflict. This means that the net resources at each organisation's command including the number of professional and support personnel, and non-labour resources, are unrelated to their effectiveness or efficiency in reducing conflict. Second, while there are well-intentioned and highly motivated people who work for these organisations without expecting (or wanting) high financial compensation, there are also others who would be more willing and able to work to reduce conflict, within *or outside,* these organisations if they could be adequately rewarded for doing so.

Targeting violent political conflict

A successful regime aimed at reducing violent political conflict should be flexible enough to choose from a large array of programmes according to the nature of the threat. No formulaic approach is going to work. What prevents conflict in one region at one time, could generate conflict in another. Bodies charged with preventing conflict should be free to choose from a wide range of options.

It is in this context that we need to consider the question of resources. Conflict prevention appears to be one poorly resourced area. Only a handful of agencies or programs have explicitly added conflict prevention to their mandate, including the UN Secretariat. This may be because or a sense of fatalism: a sense that conflict is inevitable, so why bother trying to prevent it? But it may also be a result of the inefficiency of current conflict prevention methods. Since they are so ineffective, it is rational to channel limited resources into other areas, where they will bring about a better return. It follows that increasing efficiency, as measured by conflict-reduction per unit outlay would bring double benefits: the efficiencies could be valuable in their own right, but they would also lead to more resources being deployed to reduce conflict in the future.

Our quick look at root causes and conflict prevention makes clear that policies attempting to reduce conflict must be capable of adapting to diverse and changing circumstances. They must subordinate both its intellectual approach and any institutional structures to the reduction of conflict. In other words, *the desired outcome should drive the policies and their funding,* not the other way round.

Inadequacy of current methods

Climate change and violent political conflict are extremely complex, global issues. Policies that work in one set of circumstances might be ineffective or counterproductive at a global level. Cutting back greenhouse gas emissions in Europe or the US, for instance, could simply transfer gas-emitting processes to the developing world. Increased wealth can generate more pollution, or it can encourage people to care more for the environment. A country that tolerates the production and export of armaments may be precipitating or aggravating violent conflict in other parts of the world. Or, by exporting weapons that can be used defensively, it could be stimulating peace-building initiatives. The important point is that there is currently no direct incentive for anyone to investigate these possible relationships; still less for anyone to do anything to use their knowledge of such relationships to reduce conflict. This sensitivity of cause and effect to particular circumstances cries out for alternatives to the cumbersome ways in which our international bureaucracies are currently trying, and failing, to solve them. Climate change and violent political conflict threaten us all: we cannot afford to adhere to outdated ideas or ideologies that stand in the way of their solution.

Why investigate global problems?

Offering a solution, or as I would prefer, a 'meta-solution', to the serious global challenges of climate change and violent political conflict, leaves one open to the criticism of being too idealistic. After all, countless great minds have tried and failed to bring about world peace. Very large numbers of scientists have studied climate change and believe that Kyoto, though flawed and insufficient in itself, is a crucial first step on the road to a solution. To which, I would answer: yes, but…such intellects did not organise our food industry, our clothing industry, our household goods industries. These, for the most part, are left to the private sector, within legal and ethical constraints. It is market incentives and the large pool of potential investors and employees in these businesses that combine to organise the very complex supply of these goods to those who want them and can afford to pay for them. So, I believe, it should be with the even more critical goals of climate stability and peace. Enlarging the pool of people with incentives to achieve them could succeed where some doubtless very talented, but limited in number, individuals are failing.

There are other pragmatic reasons for giving priority to global concerns in preference to more local problems:

First, possible global catastrophes, whether caused by climate change, or violent political conflict, are obviously important in their own right. They could be calamitous to many millions, and existing solutions seem doomed to fail.

Second, dealing with the global concerns of climate change or violent political conflict would alleviate other problems, such as hunger, homelessness and disease. It could do this directly by removing the causes of such problems. Or it could do so indirectly, by enabling more resources to be switched into solving such problems.

Third, it is with the global issues that the gap between what natural persons would wish for, and what they believe they can achieve through the political process, is widest, and appears to be widening. Our institutional mechanisms seem to be incapable of dealing effectively with them. In solving these problems we may be able to apply similar techniques as effectively to national, regional and local social and environmental problems.

That there is a need for new approaches to these less-than-global concerns should be clear from our discussion in Chapter 1 and above. We shall just content ourselves here with a couple of representative examples, which are important in their own right, from the rich countries. Bear in mind that these societies are the richest ever in history, that their governments spend around 40 per cent of their national income and that they squander billions of dollars annually on perverse subsidies.

Health

There are myriad ways in which national public health care funding can be allocated. Public sector health bodies have to make these resource allocation decisions on the basis of data that are necessarily incomplete. They can never know in detail the effect that spending on, say, cancer diagnostic machinery will have on the overall health of the nation, as compared with subsidising the cost of nicotine chewing gum. Neither do they have much incentive to find out. So we see a proliferation of 'health' targets, which actually have little to do with maximising welfare. Resources are allocated according to criteria that have little to do with where they will most cost-effectively improve outcomes. Consider the British National Health Service's terminal-care budget: 95 per cent of this is allocated to the 25 per cent of the UK's population who die from cancer, and just 5 per cent to the 75 per cent who die from all other causes.[62]

Such idiosyncratic decision-making is replicated and magnified at the international level. The World Health Organization (WHO) is targeting smoking and obesity.

> Spending western taxpayers' money on removing Coca-Cola vending machines from schools, and placing anti-smoking billboards in African cities, are strange priorities when every five seconds an African child dies of preventable Aids, TB or malaria.[63]

One might think that the WHO should concentrate on diseases of poverty, rather than western concerns such as obesity and smoking. Smoking and over-eating may have public health aspects to them but they are largely individual lifestyle choices, rather than involuntary causes of death.

Education

Nearly four out of 10 adults in some parts of England cannot read or write properly or do simple sums according to a Basic Skills Agency's report in May 2000. This report came a year after the agency's chairman Sir Claus Moser's report, which described the serious problem of 20 per cent of adults being "functionally illiterate".[64]

Summary

Just because a government spends so many more millions of dollars on implementing the Kyoto Protocol, or on health, education or social welfare doesn't mean it's doing anything useful:

> Thus far, the climate convention is not protecting the climate, the biodiversity convention is not protecting biodiversity, the desertification convention is not preventing desertification, and even the older and stronger Convention on the Law of the Sea is not protecting fisheries.[64.5]

When looking at social well-being what is important are outcomes. Money spent by a particular government department doesn't necessarily improve things—it is an input, not an outcome. Too often it is current institutional structures that drive policy. Politicians, officials and, very often, the media lose sight of what society actually wants. Small class sizes are not a policy goal: 100 per cent literacy and numeracy is. Shorter hospital waiting lists are not a goal: better health outcomes are. More spending on the police force is not a goal: reduced crime is. Most important of all, economic growth is not an end in itself; it is perhaps a necessary condition for achieving what we really want: a healthier, happier society, but it is certainly not sufficient. Society can agree more easily on ends than alleged means. A more rational resource allocation regime would be driven by clear, explicit *outcomes*—not inputs, activities, institutions or empty ritualistic gestures.

We need policies that are adaptive to different regions and responsive to changing circumstances. We need policies whose *objectives* are stable over time, so that people can make long-term plans and allocate resources efficiently. We need policies that are transparent, so that people know where their tax dollars are being allocated, and what sort of trade-offs their representatives are making. But most fundamentally of all, we need policies that have as their explicit objectives, improved outcomes for natural persons.

3

Organisations and objectives

*[W]e prefer to take our chance of cholera and the rest
than be bullied into health*

—a leading article from the (London) 'Times', 1 August 1854,
in response to government measures to provide basic sanitation.

We must be careful not to exaggerate the failures of government policy in the developed countries. They instituted basic health and education for their own populations. They provided other public goods, such as law and order, and sanitation. And they did so with great success and sometimes, as the quote above shows, against strident opposition.

Successful targeting

Policymaking by governments and other large organisations is inevitably geared toward achieving objectively verifiable measures and targets. Policymakers can identify problems in a society of more than a few hundred only by quantifying them. They have to use numbers to monitor progress toward their solution. A national government cannot really tell how we are feeling. It requires quantifiable data. Much of this is to the point: figures that show reduced infant mortality and higher basic literacy and numeracy figures, for example, do correlate strongly with society's well-being.

But it is mainly at lower levels of real income that the correlation between a quantifiable indicator and social welfare is strong and therefore valid as a guide

34

to policymakers.[65] [66] The case for a decent sanitation infrastructure is stronger than that for broadband internet provision. The poor are also most in need of government intervention. Eradicating poverty therefore is a valid goal that is meaningful to natural persons. If government were single-minded about improving indicators of basic health, housing or educational achievement, it would achieve the maximum benefit per dollar of taxpayer's outlay, to the great benefit of the most disadvantaged members of society.

It is at higher levels of income that numerical targeting can be futile or even counterproductive. One of the current UK Government's policy objectives, for example, is putting 50 per cent of Britain's under-30s into higher education. Like many such targets it sounds worthwhile at first. One might pause for thought though, and ask why 50 per cent? Wouldn't 66 per cent be better? Or 75 per cent? Even the 50 per cent target means, in effect, helping non-academic types go on university courses to which they are unsuited and which do very little for their career chances. Neither has past expansion of tertiary education done a great deal to benefit the disadvantaged. It makes employers unnecessarily demanding of job applicants. 'In every developed country, expanding higher education has done less for equal opportunity than one might expect—whilst steering large subsidies towards the middle classes.'[67] Worst of all, perhaps, more funding for higher education means less for literacy and numeracy programmes. There is, of course, nothing wrong with people doing whatever courses they want. But it is highly questionable whether people should be subsidised to do so from a finite educational budget when, for example, about 100 000 children leave school each year in the UK without functional literacy skills[68] and 'eight million people are so poor at reading and writing that they cannot cope with the demands of modern life.'[69]

Agriculture—a never-failing source of madcap policies—provides another example: in 2001 the incoming German Agriculture Minister announced in her maiden speech plans to increase the share of organic farming in German agriculture from 2.5 to 20 per cent over ten years.[70] As with much of the rest of agricultural policy in the rich countries these intentions will almost certainly take the form of significant transfers of resources from the poor who spend more of their income on food, to rich farmers and middle-class consumers. Why not reduce the billions of dollars that subsidise overproduction and intensify the pressure on the environment and on food safety? Again, there is nothing actually wrong with organic agriculture, though many of the claims made on its behalf do seem to be overstated.[71] But there is surely something unworthy of a government that seeks to impose arbitrary numerical targets for unstated or nebulous reasons that have nothing to do with improvements in social welfare.

Other examples are recycling targets, adopted with enthusiasm, at least at first, by many countries and local authorities. In many cases recycling is helpful to the environment; but there are instances when it probably is not. One life cycle analysis estimated that the manufacture of paper cups consumed 36 times as much electricity and more than 500 times as much wastewater as the manufacture of much-derided polystyrene foam cups.[72] Another study found that while disposable nappies (diapers) create around twice as much trash by volume as recyclable cloth nappies, they are probably more friendly to the environment, consuming less energy than, and half as much water as, cloth nappies. They also generate 40 per cent less air pollution, and 86 per cent less water pollution.[73] Perhaps that's why many recycling programmes are little more than pageants, devoid of environmental significance, where concerned households assiduously sort their rubbish into colour-coded bin bags only to find out later that all the bags were thrown onto the same landfill once they were safely out of view.[74]

It appears, to summarise, that when government supplies goods and services it does best when it tries to meet basic needs. It is only at a basic level, for example, that expenditure on public health is strongly correlated with higher social welfare, in the form of reduced morbidity, lower death rates and reduced infant mortality. At the basic level of health or education or whatever, the relationship between cause and effect, or policy and outcome, is often much easier to identify. Perhaps government's success at the basic level has led it to adopt the same approach in areas where it is not so effective. The relationship between a government's energy policy, say, and environmental outcomes is not at all clear—or at least it is obscure enough, or can be obscured easily enough, to confer plausible deniability on those responsible.

So some numerical targets are clearly inadequate, while other components of social welfare, especially at higher income levels, are too subjective for useful targeting by government. Yet there are goals that would raise social welfare and that do lend themselves to targeting, but that remain untargeted. Examples include improved basic levels of education and health, but also reduced violence at the local, national and global levels, and mitigation of such potentially disastrous environmental concerns as climate change. All have objectively quantifiable components that correlate strongly with social welfare, yet few are targeted in meaningful ways.

What we have instead is a proliferation of ineffectual government activities in peripheral areas. At the same time government fails to provide a safety net for those most in need, at home and overseas, and by failing to deal with climate change and war effectively, is quite possibly condemning many millions to death. Government should not relinquish its funding role nor its interest in social and environmental objectives; indeed, it could and should do more setting and financing of societal goals. But it could first usefully ditch some of its perverse activities and funding operations.

That it doesn't is perhaps testimony to institutional inertia.

Self-perpetuation: the unacknowledged goal

Most organisations have procedures for winding themselves up, but few willingly implement them. After foundation, they skip the existential question of whether their organisation still meets a need that arises from outside the organisation and its members. Few consider whether their resources would be better deployed outside the organisation. What happens frequently is that little by little the original purpose of the organisation fails to inform its day-to-day activities.

It is the same the world over: from schools to universities, from churches to trade union movements, from political parties to governments. Slowly, imperceptibly (at least to their staff) the organisations' actual objectives change. The stated, constitutional goals remain in place but, as the world changes, self-perpetuation becomes, by default, the real purpose of these organisations. And the way to self-perpetuation is often served by ways that have little to do with an organisation's stated purpose, or with outcomes that are meaningful to natural persons.

Take trade unions. Their focus has been on the interests of their members. But not on the interests of their members as real people, *but as workers in a particular industry or for a particular company*. Historically, when workers were more specialised and less mobile, their objective was congruent with those of their members. Thanks largely to the actions of trade unions in the past, times have changed, but the trade unions in many countries did not adapt. Individual trade unions have often acted against the longer-term interests of their own members, by making it impossible for companies or industries to stay viable. Perhaps there is little that trade unions organised according to crafts or companies that were obsolescent could do. Their members' well-being, in their capacity as natural persons, had ceased to be strongly correlated with their rewards from working in a particular role.

Government bureaucracies, government-funded agencies and other policy-making bodies can be just as prone to this sort of inertia. Their starting point is their existence as organisations, and this severely constrains their capacity to contemplate policies that threaten their role. So, for example, the swollen agricultural bureaucracies in Europe and the US will consider some re-orientation of farm subsidies, but not their abolition. Organisations resist changes that jeopardise their role, even those that might be in the long-term interests of the natural persons they are supposed to represent. This can entrench people who depend on welfare bureaucracy in their roles as supplicants, because that is what ensures the continued survival of the bureaucrat. There need not be anything inevitable about this: it is an observation rather than a law, but it does tend to apply to organisations of all sorts, including government and non-profit organisations, as well as trade unions, churches, schools or religious and social organisations.

It is especially unfortunate that organisational self-perpetuation seems to take precedence even when it is realised that outcomes—results—are what really matter. The recent bureaucratic history of the New Zealand and US Governments shows that this does happen.

Example 1: Subordination to institutional structures: New Zealand state sector reform

Over several years beginning in 1988, New Zealand's public sector was radically and innovatively reformed. Tightly held central control gave way to autonomous departments, headed by chief executives with the authority to take decisions relating to the whole of their organisations. Chief executives are now expected to hire and fire staff, negotiate pay, manage their finances and capital assets, negotiate purchase agreements and be held to account for outputs. In the New Zealand public sector:

- accountability for resources and results is maintained through contestable, contract-like arrangements within government,

- performance agreements between government ministers and chief executives lay down standards and expectations for department heads, and

- purchase agreements between ministers and departments specify the outputs to be produced during the year.

The arrangements between ministers and departments specify *ex ante* the outputs they are required to deliver, but leave chief executives free to select the mix of inputs to be used in producing these outputs. This system has been extended to encompass the specification of, and accountability for, longer-term objectives. Since 1994 the New Zealand Government has defined the medium-term outcomes it is trying to achieve in nine 'strategic result areas' (SRAs) and linked the outputs delivered by each department to these SRAs through 'key result areas', which form the basis of their performance agreements.

What have the results been? According to a report commissioned by the New Zealand Government, there have been efficiency gains. However, the transactions costs incurred in negotiating agreements, monitoring compliance and preparing reports have been high, and in many cases have 'soaked up a substantial part of the efficiency gains' made from restructuring.[75]

In the context of bureaucratic change the New Zealand reforms were radical. But the reforms were constrained by the then existing institutional structures. At the outset of the reform programme, government departments had been envisaged as achieving specific *outcomes*. But that vision did not carry through.

Instead, outputs became the measure by which departments' performance is judged. One reason is said to be the self-interest of ministers and public servants, who are unwilling to be scrutinised.[76] Another is that while the supply of outputs can be directly attributed to departments' performance, outcomes can be influenced by factors beyond their control. As one commentator put it:

'outcomes are externalities in two-party relationships; therefore it is exceed-ingly difficult to assign responsibility for them.'[77]

So what happened? It looks very much as though the perceived need to assign responsibility in effect hijacked more thoroughgoing reform. The perception of such a need arises only because the players—those whose responsibility is to be assigned—are known in advance and are assumed constant.

And who are these players? Why, they are the existing government depart-ments, of course. In effect the New Zealand reforms have *subordinated results to an assumed need to assign responsibility*, which in turn seems to be driven by existing institutional structures and their wish to remain in control.

Example 2: the United States

Concerned that the US federal government was more focused on programme activities and processes than outcomes, the US Congress passed the Govern-ment Performance and Results Act ('Results Act') of 1993. The Act 'seeks to improve the management of federal programs by shifting the focus of deci-sion-making from staffing and activity levels to the results of federal pro-grams.'[78] It requires federal agencies to develop strategic plans, with long-term, outcome-orientated goals, annual goals linked to achieving the long-term goals, and annual reports on the results achieved.

After ten years, what has been the result? In March 2004, the United States General Accounting Office (GAO) published its assessment.[79] There have been cultural changes within government agencies. Federal managers are now informed by significantly more outcome-oriented performance measures. Goals are both more quantifiable and results-oriented. There is a greater focus on performance measurement, orientation toward outcomes rather than inputs and outputs, and an increased focus on programme evaluation.[80]

All this is very good news. But the GAO report points to certain implementa-tion problems. Importantly, there is no real co-ordination of an agency's annual performance goals with broader strategic goals.[81] And:

> ...in certain areas, *federal managers* continue to have difficulty setting out-come-oriented goals, collecting useful data on results, and linking institu-tional, program, unit, and individual performance measurement and reward

systems. Finally, there is an inadequate focus on addressing issues that cut across federal agencies.[82] [emphasis added]

The fault, it seems to this author, lies with the way in which strategic goals are chosen. Goals are still formulated as if the existing agency structure were a given. Setting outcome-orientated goals should not be the concern of 'federal managers'. It should be a part of the political process: the agency structure should be irrelevant in deciding what outcomes to target. So we find that institutional structures still limit the scope of reform.

> Mission fragmentation and overlap contribute to difficulties in addressing crosscutting issues, particularly when those issues require a national focus, such as homeland security, drug control, and the environment. GPRA requires a governmentwide performance plan, where these issues could be addressed in a centralized fashion, but OMB has not issued a distinct plan since 1999.[83]

Looking in particular at health, we can see how institutional structures can be a distraction from broad outcomes insofar as agencies tailor their activities to what they have done in the past and what they are best suited to do. It was in 1979 that the US Public Health Service (PHS) first set national health goals.[84] Goals to be achieved by 1990 included a 35 per cent reduction in infant mortality, a 20 per cent reduction in childhood deaths, a 20 per cent death rate reduction for adolescents and young adults, and 25 per cent death rate reduction for adults aged 25 to 64 years. For persons over the age of 65, the aim was reduce the number of disability days, with the goal of improving the quality of life for older adults.

It is difficult to fault such objectives. There is more: for the next stage, the PHS developed papers on 15 disease prevention and priority health promotion areas. After consultation with 167 experts, draft objectives were circulated to more than 2000 organisations and individuals for review and comment. The result of this collaboration was *Promoting Health/Preventing Disease: Objectives for the Nation*, published in 1980.[85] This set 226 objectives with targets for achievement by 1990, and laid the foundation for a similar exercise ten years later. A draft of objectives to be achieved by the year 2000 was released in September 1989. Public comment was invited and used to create a consensus document, *Healthy People 2000*,[86] which launched a 10-year national initiative to improve the health of all Americans.

> This collaboration of States, academics, private and voluntary organizations, and interested individuals ensured that the goals and objectives of *Healthy People 2000* are not simply those of the Federal government but are national in scope. The combined efforts of the public and private sectors are requisite to these targets being achieved.[87]

And

> A comparison of the 1989 draft of the objectives with the final 1990 publication does show that substantial revisions were made based on public comment.[88]

In choosing over-arching strategic outcomes and in consulting with experts and the public this is an excellent start. It shows that it is quite realistic it is to expect valuable contributions from the public when policy is expressed in terms of broad, targeted outcomes.

A crucial flaw, however, is the small role given to efficiency in achieving targeted outcomes. This applies not only to the Healthy People Program, but to the entire Results Act initiative. While US agencies have begun to establish a link between results and resources,[89]

> [u]nfortunately, most existing federal performance appraisal systems are not designed to support a meaningful performance-based pay system in that they fail to link institutional, program, unit, and individual performance measurement and reward systems....Managers also identified difficulties in distinguishing between the results produced by the federal program and results caused by external factors or non-federal actors.... Finally, agency officials believe that Congress could make greater use of performance information to conduct oversight and to inform appropriations decisions. [90]

The GAO found that only one of the six agencies that it looked in more detail clearly linked its costs of the achievement of outcomes.[91]

One difficulty, the GAO reports, is that it is difficult to establish outcome-based performance measures when the programme, or 'line of effort', is not easily quantifiable. 'In some agencies, particularly those that have a research and development component, managers reported difficulties in establishing meaningful outcome measures.'[92]

A second difficulty identified by the GAO is that the federal budget is allocated on an agency-by-agency basis, so it does not provide 'the integrated perspective of government performance envisioned by GPRA'.[93] It would be better if the budget were allocated according to crosscutting theme. As the GAO put it

> The development of a set of key national indicators could be used as a basis to inform the development of governmentwide strategic and annual performance plans.[94]

Indeed, the GAO goes on to recommend that there should be a government-wide performance plan.[95]

As in New Zealand, then, we see that existing institutional structures constrain a truly outcome-based policy. Outcome measures for bodies engaged in long-term activities, for example, research and development, should be subsumed into broader strategic goals. It should not be up to the government or a government agency to monitor how efficient agencies are in achieving sub-objectives. More crucially, the resource allocation should not be on an agency basis. Resources, ideally, would shift in and out of different activities depending on how efficient each activity is in contributing to the achievement of the strategic goals.

There is no question that the GPRA does represent a big step forward for outcome-orientated government. It appears that progress is being impeded, however, by the overly large influence of existing institutions in deciding how resources aimed at achieving specified outcomes are to be allocated.

The unimportance of outcomes

When looking at policymaking bodies, what is particularly striking is, with the partial exception of the US federal government, how unimportant outcomes are in determining both how policy is made, and who makes it.

> ...policies are often adopted on the basis of less careful analysis than their importance warrants, leaving wide room for mistakes and misperceptions. Forces of knowledge destruction are often stronger than those favoring knowledge creation. Hence states have an inherent tendency toward primi-

tive thought, and the conduct of public affairs is often polluted by myth, misinformation, and flimsy analysis.[96]

In our complex economies, outcomes can be difficult to trace accurately to the events and people that generated them. Our extreme specialisation increases the length of the chain between producers and consumers and the time lags between cause and effect. Moreover, it increases people's alienation from each other, particularly between policymakers and stakeholders. The result is that appearances, personalities, and emotional appeal assume a great importance.

> Therapeutic politics eschews matters of policy and principle and attempts to establish a point of contact in the domain of the emotion with an otherwise estranged electorate..... The shift in rhetoric from standing up for what is 'right' to upholding what one feels good about signifies the incorporation of emotionalism into the heart of political decision-making.[97]

Of course, under the current system and, with the exception perhaps of a handful of academics and policy zealots, nobody has a very compelling interest in impartial exploration of the relationships between policies and outcomes. Most people who make and implement policy work for bodies—usually government agencies—that do not reward people for their success in achieving stated policy goals. So there is very little incentive to discover which activities are most effective in achieving social and environmental objectives is missing. This perhaps is the key to effective policymaking.

4

Towards a solution: outcomes, incentives and markets

In general, and with few exceptions, government policies:

- reward people, activities or institutions, rather than outcomes;

- have objectives that are unstated, uncosted, obscure or conflicting; and

- do not reward those who achieve social and environmental goals in ways that are correlated with their effectiveness.

These failings apply to national, regional and local governments, and to international bodies such as the United Nations.

We all see the results. One is the persistence of social and environmental problems, while at the same time military spending remains at very high levels and, against all economic rationality, wasteful policies such as perverse subsidies continue. These, we have seen, benefit only a few favoured corporate bodies at the expense of the vast majority of a country's citizens, the environment and would-be producers outside the subsidising economy. This mad extravagance persists while at the same time many of society's least advantaged members slip through the gaping holes in governments' health and education programmes. And at the same time, the rich countries and the entire world population, are threatened by global catastrophe that could arise from climate change, other environmental threats, or the proliferation of weapons of mass destruction.

A symptom of this malaise is the disengagement of many from the political process. Even the United Kingdom's Labour Party's 'landslide' majority in the British House of Commons is not what it seems. Labour received just over 40 per cent of the vote in 2002, with a 60 per cent turnout. So only 24 per cent of the electorate actually voted for Tony Blair's party. In the US President George W Bush received votes from fewer than a quarter of the voting age population. It is the same in most other western democracies. We have begun to accept that whichever party receives 25 per cent of the popular vote has 'won' the election. In most countries, this represents a dramatic decline in popular engagement with politics over the past few decades.[98]

Perhaps one reason for this is that people are sceptical about the ability of the different political parties to deliver. In the absence of any great ideological divide, most parties have approximately the same manifesto at election time, and seem equally (in)capable of achieving results that are meaningful to electors. If such voter apathy co-existed with satisfaction or optimism about the political environment it would not be a worry. But unfortunately it goes hand-in-hand with deepening dissatisfaction, cynicism and even despair, at the ability of our politicians to deal with urgent domestic and global concerns.

Targeting specified outcomes that are meaningful to natural persons, as the US Results Act begins to do, is a necessary first step, but it is not sufficient. The other necessary step is to ensure that resources are allocated in ways that can most cost-effectively achieve these outcomes. This is where market incentives come into the picture.

Incentives and markets

Democratic governments do a reasonable job at representing and articulating their people's wishes. Where they are not so successful is in working out the most efficient ways of achieving these goals. This achievement is really a matter of allocating scarce resources. In economic theory, and on all the evidence, markets are the best way of allocating scarce resources to achieve prescribed ends.

When the distance between government and people is large, as it is in our highly specialised economies, government decisions about resource allocation are essentially central planning. Central planners think they know best how to solve economic, social and environmental problems, and most government policies embody this assumption. One or a few modish concepts tend to dominate. Central planning is ponderous, uniform and slow to adapt, while the sort of complex issues—climate change, violent political conflict, crime and poverty—that we are discussing need exactly the opposite approach. Identifying these problems and funding their solution might need a global or national body, but actually solving them requires pluralism not central planning.

And markets are pluralist. Markets encourage people and firms to try different approaches, and also to assess the results of these approaches. Markets also hold people accountable for the results and ensure that ineffective or counterproductive approaches are terminated once they are seen to have failed. They call on a phenomenal information-processing power that central planners simply cannot emulate.

Unfortunately, many believe that market forces must inevitably conflict with social goals. Understandably so, since in recent decades deregulation of some economies and an enhanced role for markets have made some people very wealthy indeed, while the less well-off have gained relatively little and many social and environmental problems appear to have worsened.

So it is important to remind ourselves that market forces and self-interest can serve public, as well as private, goals. Often, these private goals coincide with social goals, so that, for instance, the market routinely performs vital tasks such as food distribution and the provision of such indispensables as home medicines, baby needs, furniture and other consumer goods. These are exceedingly complex tasks but, left to the multiplicity of agents operating in reasonably competitive markets, they are accomplished in ways that fulfil not only the private goals of the firms and consumers involved but also society's goal of efficient supply of goods and services. This feat results from the combination of the self-interest of large numbers of market players, and their ability to react appropriately to ever-changing circumstances. Some would attribute the triumph of the western market economies over the state-controlled, centrally-planned economies of the Soviet Union and its satellites to the victory of materialist motivations over political ideals. But it is more likely that the efficiencies and incentives of pluralism had won out over central direction; that decentralisation had triumphed over dirigisme.[99]

Governments tend to be centralist in their instincts. In practice, this has meant that market forces are rarely allowed to play a significant role in organising the production and distribution of those goods and services that governments supply. Government agencies also operate in a non-competitive environment, which discourages self-evaluation.[100] Since the governments of the developed countries now spend on average of around 40 per cent of their economies' national income, these are significant deficiencies. One result is that public services, such as health, education and housing, seem perpetually to be in crisis. Another is that large sums of consumers' and taxpayers' money are, as we have seen, wasted on perverse subsidies to sectors such as agriculture, road transport and energy.

The manifold complexity of violent political conflict or of environmental challenges such as climate change, the proliferation of intricate, obscure relationships between cause and effect: all aspects of our social and environmental problems cry out for a pluralist solution. No single approach, and no planning by a single body, however large, is going to work. We need to find a way of ensuring that the pluralism evoked by market forces allocates the resources we devote to accomplishing our social and environmental goals, and that any organisations that might arise are entirely subordinated to the achievement of these goals.

5

Social Policy Bonds

Introduction

War, terrorism, climate change: many of our most urgent social and environmental problems are too complex for any except specialists fully to comprehend. Even the specialists often disagree, and not only on peripheral matters. They may be predisposed to select only the information that suits their ideology. Social and environmental problems involve so many relationships, so many variables, and such large distances of time and space between cause and effect, that to disinterested observers, there are good cases to be made on both sides of arguments about how to solve them.

Rather than wait till scientific or political arguments are resolved, or to pursue some abstract notions of justice in matters of human conflict, we might do better on efficiency grounds, to subordinate all our activities to our intended outcomes: climate stability, for example, or conflict reduction.

Social Policy Bonds take that approach. They would reward people only when they actually achieve targeted social or environmental goals. A fixed number of Social Policy Bonds ('bonds') would be issued. The bonds could be issued and backed by local or national government, by non-governmental organisations, by global bodies such as the United Nations, or by private individuals. They would initially be auctioned to the highest bidders. The bonds' backers would undertake to redeem these bonds for a fixed sum *only when a specified social objective has been achieved*. The bonds would not bear interest. They would be freely tradeable after issue, and their market value would rise and fall. Social

Policy Bonds would therefore differ from conventional bonds in that they would have an uncertain redemption date which, in combination with a fixed redemption value, implies an uncertain yield: holders would raise their bonds' yield by achieving the targeted objective quickly. Once the targeted outcome had been achieved, whoever backed the bonds would redeem them. The rest of this chapter outlines the essential elements of a bond regime. Subsequent chapters look in more detail at their operational aspects.

How would Social Policy Bonds work? They would create an interest group—bondholders—who have powerful incentives to achieve the targeted social objective efficiently and quickly, or to pay others to do so. Consider an example. Assume that an urban authority is prepared to spend a maximum of say $10 million to reduce the crime rate within its borders by 50 per cent. It issues one million bonds that become worth $10 when the crime rate falls below 50 per cent of current levels for a sustained period—say one year. Because the market would see this objective as unlikely to be achieved in the near future, it would put a low value on the bonds when they are floated. Assume successful bidders pay as little as $1 for each of the bonds. (This sum would be held by the issuing authority partially to offset the cost of redemption of the bonds.) Now, they hold an asset that could appreciate in value by 900 per cent if a sustained halving of the crime rate were achieved. This provides the motivation for bondholders to do what they can to reduce the crime rate.

Social Policy Bonds could in principle, be used to solve any social or environmental problem that can be reliably defined and quantified. Key criteria for policy areas within which Social Policy Bonds would show the most marked improvement over current programmes are:

1. existing policies have objectives that are unstated, uncosted, obscure or conflicting;

2. financial rewards to those involved in achieving objectives are uncorrelated to their effectiveness in doing so;

3. a wide array of diverse, adaptive approaches may be necessary; and

4. our knowledge of the problem, its causes and solutions, is scanty and improving all the time.

Sadly many social and environmental problems fit all of these criteria. Climate change and violent political conflict are the most urgent, global concerns, but there are also examples at national and local level including crime prevention, health, education, and air, water and noise pollution.

Markets minimise costs

Whoever issues Social Policy Bonds could estimate the maximum value of the targeted outcome. One consideration would be the financial impact of solving a social problem. Achieving certain social goals would actually bring about financial savings for a government. For instance, when the number of unemployed claimants comes down, the state saves unemployment benefit and gains an increase in income tax for each person who is taken off the unemployment register and goes into gainful employment. Achieving this particular social goal could therefore generate a net fiscal benefit, even in the short term. For other targeted objectives, such as a lower crime rate, there would also be positive, but less easily quantifiable, net financial benefits, and these may take longer to arise. Other social goals, such as reduced rates of homelessness, or increases in literacy, might increase monetary returns to the government in the long term, but would certainly generate very little net revenue in the short run. And there would be many social or environmental goals whose achievement would impose net financial costs on society in the foreseeable future.

But people and their governments want things other than for financial reasons. A society in which everybody can read, in which people feel safer from crime and breathe clean air is surely desirable in its own right. Government and society have to decide on how far we pursue these objectives, and how valuable they are. They would have to take into account both the financial and nonfinancial benefits in deciding on the maximum value of each social goal, in advance of issuing the bonds. A bond regime would make this a simpler and more transparent task than the current array of social policies, because people would be asked to value outcomes, rather than activities intended to achieve these outcomes. If Social Policy Bonds were to be used in conjunction with other policy instruments to achieve the same goal, government would also have to decide on the proportion of total expenditure that would be spent on the bond component. These factors would determine how many bonds it would issue for a definite redemption value. The maximum cost to the government of the bond issue would (ignoring administration costs) equal: the total number of bonds issued multiplied by their redemption value, minus any revenues gained on floating the bonds.

Though it would have to decide on the *maximum* cost to society of achieving the objective, a government issuing Social Policy Bonds would not have to work out how much the *actual* cost would be with any accuracy. That would be done by bidders for the bonds in the open market. Assume again that bonds were to be used exclusively in pursuit of a 50 per cent reduction in the crime rate, and that the urban authority issues one million bonds, of redemption value $10.00. If the market decided that the issue value of these bonds were $1.00, the net cost to the issuers of achieving the targeted objective (ignoring administration costs) would be $9 million. In other words, the market at the time of issue believes that the cost, including its profit margin, of achieving the objective would be $9 million.

Now suppose the bond issuers are completely in the dark about how much it will cost to achieve a targeted objective and instead of issuing one million bonds they issue ten million with the same redemption value, $10.00. They would then be liable for a maximum cost of $100 million. However, the market would still reckon that it could achieve the objective for around $9 million. So instead of valuing the bonds at $1.00 competition between potential investors would bid up the issue price of the bonds to around $9.10. (Social Policy Bonds would be an unusual financial instrument, in that the more that were issued, the higher would be their value!) *The issuers therefore would not have to estimate with any accuracy how much a targeted objective might cost to achieve, and they would put a cap on their total liability by limiting the number of bonds issued.*

So the Social Policy Bond mechanism ensures that the market, which means people *other than a handful of government employees*, would decide roughly how much it would cost to reach a specified social outcome. They would do this when they bid for the bonds at issue *and at all times afterwards*. This fact, and the would-be bondholders' incentive to minimise their costs, contrast with the current system in which the costs of achieving particular outcomes, if they are calculated at all, are not widely known, nor subject to competitive bidding. Under the current system, in fact, many of the people charged with achieving social goals (or, more likely, with supplying certain outputs) have every incentive to inflate the projected cost of their doing so. Under a bond regime, however, the awesome information-processing power of the market would be channelled into minimising the costs of achieving these goals.

Note that the issuing body could add to the number of bonds in circulation after floating at any time, if it wanted to boost the efforts going into achieving a particular social goal. If it wanted, for whatever reason, to *reduce* such efforts, the situation would be a little more complicated. It could buy bonds back from holders, but doing so would reduce the total funds to be spent on achieving the targeted objective, and so would lower the value of all bonds in circulation. People might therefore be unwilling to buy bonds in the first place if they thought there were a high probability of the issuing body's buying some of them back in this way. They would demand some sort of premium for taking that risk. Alternatively, the issuing body could undertake either that it would never buy Social Policy Bonds back or that, if it did, it would pay the market price ruling before it announced its purchase intentions.

What would bondholders do?

Social Policy Bonds would rely on the people or institutions that hold bonds initiating or facilitating programmes that promote the targeted objective. Bondholders could use their own capital, or borrow on the strength of the redemption value of their bonds. They would have an incentive to cooperate with each other to help reduce crime, and to do so as cost-effectively as possible. These people's motivation would come from the expected capital gain they would enjoy as the bond price rises in line with the enhanced probability that the objective will be achieved early.

Consider some of the measures that active investors in bonds targeting the crime rate could put into operation:

- encouraging neighbourhood watch schemes,
- encouraging parents to monitor their children's activities more closely,
- subsidising recruitment of unemployed workers, or
- complementing police patrols with private security patrols.

In many countries, some arm of government already undertakes one or more of these activities. And some longer-term projects, like research into the causes of crime, are done by private bodies or universities, independently of government or with only a small contribution from government funds. The crucial difference a Social Policy Bond regime would make is that people would have incentives to seek out and develop those ways of reducing crime that are most cost-effective. A police force, a bureaucracy, or an academic criminology department, however well-intentioned, is not currently rewarded in ways that correlate with its success in achieving society's objectives—even if these are explicitly targeted. But under a Social Policy Bond regime the self-interest of bondholders would act so as to encourage those ways of reducing crime that would give taxpayers the best return for their outlay. These ways may have been tried before, or tried in different cities, or they may be new and untried. Bondholders would be motivated to seek out, invent and deploy the most efficient methods for the city or country whose crime rate is targeted.

Bondholders need not participate directly in any crime reduction projects. Their role could be one of financing such projects on the strength of the redemption value of their bonds, or on the strength of any projected increase in the value of their bonds. Their motivation would arise from the anticipated supernormal profit arising from early redemption of the bonds.

One further activity that bondholders might indulge in is lobbying government. They might press for longer prison sentences, for example, thinking that these would deter potential criminals or keep convicted criminals out of circulation. Such lobbying, of course, already goes on because government is always making decisions that create winners and losers. Under a Social Policy Bond regime the source of this sort of pressure, and the motivation for it, would be more transparent than under the current system and it need not pose any different problems. (Chapter 7 looks at the subject of lobbying in more detail.)

Trading the bonds

Social Policy Bonds, once issued and sold, must be readily tradeable at any time until redemption. The operation of such a 'secondary market' would be critical to the way Social Policy Bonds work. Many bond purchasers would want or need to sell their bonds before redemption—which might be a long time in the future. With a secondary market, these holders would be able to realise any capital appreciation experienced by their holdings of Social Policy

Bonds whenever they chose to do so. This would make the bonds a more attractive investment in the first place.

Such capital appreciation would arise from upward movements in the market price of the bonds. Of course, these prices could move in either direction. Major determinants of the bond price would include:

- how remote the market believes the targeted objective is to being achieved;

- market perceptions of risk and uncertainty; and

- the relative appeal of other investments.

These and other determinants would vary continuously with time and so would the market value of Social Policy Bonds. Note that the market's valuation of the bonds would be influenced not only by efforts that bondholders make toward achieving the targeted goal, but by external factors. Some of these could be apparent at the time of issue: for instance, one of the determinants of crime is demography. Specifically, the greater the number of young male adults, the larger the number of crimes tends to be, all other factors being equal. Demographic variables like this, and others that can be anticipated, would be factored into the market value of the bonds at issue. But other influences cannot be anticipated. So, for example, the market price of bonds targeting property crime could fall if, say, there were a string of power failures that led to looting. Or it could rise on the capture of a ringleader of a particularly successful gang of burglars or car thieves. The value of bonds targeting air pollution could rise or fall with climatic conditions, volcanic eruptions, or the price of oil or coal. The value of bonds targeting unemployment could rise or fall with financial data, such as the exchange rate (making the country a more or less attractive venue for overseas investment), or interest rates (making firms more or less likely to lay off employees).

As with other investments, risk and uncertainty would be important determinants of the bonds' market price. Bonds targeting more remote objectives (cutting crime by 80 per cent say) would be riskier than those whose outcomes were closer to current levels (cutting crime by 20 per cent). And there would also be uncertainty attached to the Social Policy Bond mechanism itself, especially when Social Policy Bonds are first issued, as they would be untried and unproven.

Like shares and other financial instruments, the prices of Social Policy Bonds would be in constant flux. New information affecting the prices would become available day by day. As well as external influences on the bond prices, people would carry out research specifically aimed at determining the value of the bonds as an investment. The effects of all these data on the bonds' market value would generate useful insights into the relationships between circumstances, events, social problems and desired outcomes.

Giving bondholders the chance to benefit from these price movements is essential. Apart from making the bonds more attractive at issue, a healthy secondary market would be important for another crucial reason: some investors may be able to speed up only one, or a few, of the processes necessary for the targeted objective to be achieved. Once these investors had made their contribution and seen the capital value of their bonds increase in line with the increased probability of the bonds' early redemption, they might have no wish to speculate on the speed at which the remaining processes would be carried out. Other groups of active investors, who could have greater expertise in performing these later processes, must be given an incentive to use their expertise to accelerate attainment of the targeted objective. The possible capital appreciation of bonds bought from previous owners and sold at a still higher price (or redeemed) would provide this incentive. The new owners, if they were successful in these later stages, would realise this capital appreciation.

Cascading incentives

As the bonds are traded, they would tend to flow towards those who were most able to help solve the targeted social problem. In fact, though, trading in the bonds would not always be necessary. Large bondholders might simply decide to subcontract out the required work to many different agents, while they themselves would hold the bonds from issue to redemption. The important point is that the bond mechanism would ensure that the people who allocate the finance had an incentive to do so efficiently and to reward successful outcomes, rather than merely to pay people for undertaking an activity. At the limit, just one single investor could buy all the bonds. If this buyer were determined to hold on to the bonds until redemption, then the bonds would function as a sort of performance-related contract, with the bonds' backers paying out only when the objective had been achieved. The buyer could contract out most, or all, of the work required to achieve the objective, with the incentives generated by the bonds for speedy accomplishment cascading down from the bondholder to those subcontracted to do the work. If this bondholder, for whatever reason, were to become inefficient in pursuit of that objective, or were simply to lose interest in it, then he or she could simply sell the bonds to more efficient and more highly motivated investors.

Too large a number of small bondholders would probably do little to help solve targeted social problems by themselves. If there were many small hold- ers, it is likely that the value of their bonds would fall until there were aggrega- tion of holdings by people or institutions large enough to initiate effective problem-solving projects. In much the same way as share privatisation issues the world over have turned out, the bonds would probably end up mainly in the hands of large holders, be they individuals or institutions. Between them, these large holders could account for the majority of bond holding. Even these bodies might not be big enough, on their own, to achieve much without the cooperation of other bondholders. They might also resist initiating projects until they could be sure that other holders would not be 'free riders' (see Chapter 7). So there would be a powerful incentive for all bondholders to *cooperate with each other* to help solve the targeted problem. They would share the same interest in seeing targeted objectives achieved quickly. So they would share information, trade bonds with each other and collaborate on objective- achieving projects. They would also set up payment systems to ensure that people, bondholders or not, were mobilised to help achieve targeted objec- tives. Bondholders would either trade bonds, or make incentive payments to ensure that any proceeds from higher bond prices, or from redemption, would be channelled in ways most likely to stimulate speedy achievement of the tar- geted objective. Large bondholders, in cooperation with each other, would be able to set up such systems cost-effectively.

Regardless of who actually owns the bonds, aggregation of holdings and the cooperation of large bondholders would ensure that people who help achieve social goals were rewarded in ways that maximise their efficiency.

Objectives and indicators

For a Social Policy Bond regime to be effective, clarity and transparency of objectives are essential. The targeted objective must be *carefully defined* so that targeted changes either actually are, or are strongly correlated with, what society wants to achieve. For instance, numbers of reported crimes could be targeted if the objective were to achieve a safer urban environment. But this indicator may be unsatisfactory if, for instance, the crime rate became so high that people did not bother to report minor assaults or burglaries to the police. A more appropriate indicator might be derived from responses to victim surveys. Because the bonds target outcomes they demand clear thinking and transparency as to exactly what it is that society is aiming to achieve. Is lower unemployment the objective? Or lower expenditure on unemployment benefit? Or higher employment? Is it worthwhile aiming to reduce, in particular, unemployment amongst 16–24 year old males? Or ethnic minorities? Or the unemployment rate in particular regions? Also note that it would generally be unsatisfactory to redeem the bonds the moment a targeted figure had been attained: the objective should be a *sustained* lower level of (say) unemployment, and that is how it would have to be defined when the bonds were issued.

Targeted objectives should also be capable of being *accurately tracked by quantifiable indicators*, whose progress accurately corresponds with progress toward the desired social outcome. As well, objectives should, in general, be as *broad* as possible, so that one particular objective cannot be achieved at the expense of other societal goals.

The last point needs elaboration. Consider the application of a bond regime to environmental problems. Assume the concentration of atmospheric lead were to be targeted by a bond issue. It might be that targeting lead in this way would cause people to increase their use of other polluting substitutes—and these could be at least as dangerous as the original levels of lead.

One way of dealing with this problem could be to aim initially at an unambitious reduction in the lead level. Depending on the effects of such a reduction on the use of offending substitutes, other bonds could then be issued, either targeting the level of lead, or targeting the level of offending substitutes. But a better approach would be to target, more comprehensively, atmospheric pollution. This could be expressed perhaps as an index of atmospheric pollutants, weighted according to their lethality and other factors (see box, *What to target?*). But perhaps the best approach of all, assuming our sole concern is human health, is to target broader health indicators, such as longevity and infant mortality, so that resources are deployed wherever their positive effects on health will be greatest.

What to target?

Breadth of objective Targeted objectives should, in principle, be as broad as possible. It would probably be unsatisfactory to make nitrates, for example, the sole target of a bond issue targeting water pollution if it were likely that farmers would respond by increasing the use of phosphates. Instead, both could be made the target of a single bond issue or, even better, water pollution itself could be targeted: Social Policy Bonds lend themselves to targeting combinations of objectives. They could target indices encompassing a wide range of pollutants, weighted according to their contribution to environmental degradation.

Ends or means? In principle ends, rather than means to ends, would make better targets for Social Policy Bonds. Thus, it would be preferable for bond issuers to target, for example, homelessness, rather than housing starts, and leave it for bondholders to decide on how best to achieve the desired goal. Similarly, it might be preferable to target not water pollution, but such indicators of environmental status as biodiversity of a river, lake or sea, perhaps in conjunction with more subjective indicators like the opinions people have about the quality of their environment, as measured by questionnaire responses. Bonds could be issued whose redemption value were on a sliding scale, reflecting the perceived adverse environmental impacts of the targeted range of pollutants.

Spatial distribution Bonds aimed at improving national averages of such indicators as pollution would be adequate sole policy instruments only if society were unconcerned about the distribution of pollutants. Otherwise bonds targeting pollution could be made redeemable only on the condition that pollutant thresholds would not breached in any part of the country concerned.

Time period Bond issues could provide bonus payments for achievement of the targeted goal by a specified date. Or issuers could stipulate that bonds would not be redeemed unless the targeted objective were achieved by a certain date, or that they would be redeemed for a sum that would diminish over the time it took for the objective to be achieved. The market would factor all such penalties or bonuses into the bond price.

Similar concerns, perhaps less clear-cut, could arise when targeting regional problems. If bonds were issued targeting the number of unemployed people of working age in northeast England, say, then bondholders might attempt to solve the problem by paying the unemployed of that region to move somewhere else. This might, of course, be seen as a social benefit. But if not, provisos could written into the bond issue, such that they would not be redeemed if the population in the north-east fell below a certain level. In general, objectives that are complementary and that, if not pursued jointly, could conflict, should be targeted by a single bond issue.

A few basic questions and answers Social Policy Bonds follow. Succeeding chapters look in more detail at the advantages and practical aspects of a bond regime.

Social Policy Bonds: questions and answers

Who would issue the Social Policy Bonds?

Local and national governments could issue Social Policy Bonds, as could international bodies such as the United Nations and World Bank. But, importantly, private individuals who feel strongly about a particular social or environmental concern could also issue Social Policy Bonds. They could call on members of the public to add to funds available for bond redemption. Purchasers of these bonds could initiate projects that complement existing activities currently undertaken by governments. A guide for private individuals interested in issuing their own Social Policy Bonds forms the Annex to this book.

Who would buy the bonds?

The most important buyers would be institutions, who would buy many of the bonds, and use the profits they anticipate from early redemption, or bond price rises, as collateral to finance projects that would help achieve the targeted social objective.

Wouldn't people just buy Social Policy Bonds, then do nothing?

If too many people failed to take any outcome-achieving activities the value of their bonds would fall, as the targeted objective became ever more remote. At some point, the market price of the bonds would fall to such a low point, that it would pay somebody to buy the bonds, and do something to help achieve the targeted objective.

What happens if Social Policy Bonds are held by many different holders? That would mean that bondholders might be tempted to do nothing, or that they are not rewarded in proportion to their efforts.

If too many Social Policy Bonds were held by would-be free riders who had no intention of doing anything to help achieve the targeted social objective, then the value of all the bonds would fall. This would lead to aggregation of bond holdings, so that most bonds would be held by relatively large owners. They would then have incentives to cooperate with each other. This would mean, amongst other things, that they would all benefit by agreeing on how the specified social problem could best be targeted. One element of the optimal strategy will be to decide who will be responsible for what activities, and how they shall be compensated. Major bondholders will certainly have incentives to share information with each other. Many of the bonds would be traded between bondholders.

But what about those with smaller holdings?

Some might think that holders of bonds representing, say, 5 per cent of all the bonds issued would be deterred from taking actions to help achieve the targeted objective because they will not be the sole beneficiaries of appreciation in the value of the bonds. This is unlikely to happen for three reasons. First, typically people do take actions that will enrich others as well as themselves. Minority shareholders and company managers, for instance, frequently initiate actions that will see major shareholders benefit far more than themselves. They might try to accumulate more shares in anticipation of their own activities, but this activity certainly does not inhibit initiatives aimed at increasing share prices. Second, the important criterion for bondholders is whether their investment in objective-achieving activities will generate a sufficient return to themselves. They will not be deterred if their activities also benefit others. Of course, if their activities are successful in achieving a specified objective, then other bondholders may replicate them, so raising the price of the bonds significantly. Third, minority bondholders could use futures or options markets, so that they would enjoy a leveraged return if their activities are successful in raising the bond price.

What happens when a targeted objective has actually been achieved? Wouldn't more bonds have to be issued to maintain the status quo?

For the bonds to be redeemed, the achievement would have to be *sustained* for a specified period. After that period, it is likely that the most successful and efficient systems developed to solve the social problem the first time will allow government to allocate less funding for maintaining or improving the new status quo. The bonds encourage *diverse* and *efficient* solutions to social problems.

Could the bonds really solve such global problems as climate change and violent political conflict?

Once the bonds have been successfully used at the local and national levels, there would be every reason to apply the principle to global problems. The thrust of the concept is to give people incentives to solve targeted problems. Too many global resources are wasted by inefficient, corrupt or malicious governments who have no wish or incentive to help solve global problems. Social Policy Bonds could undermine, co-opt, or distract those who are opposed to social goals.

6

Advantages of a Social Policy Bond regime

This chapter elaborates some of the operational aspects of Social Policy Bonds by looking at their advantages. Its main focus is on government programmes, as it is governments who currently allocate most of the financial resources that fund social and environmental programmes. Bear in mind, though, that anyone, not only taxpayers, can issue their own Social Policy Bonds for objectives that are important to them. (This book's Annex looks at privately-backed initiatives.)

Efficiency

The main likely advantage of Social Policy Bonds is that, because they would inject self-interest into all stages necessary for solving social problems, they would be *more cost-effective* than current, activity-based programmes. For the same government expenditure, therefore, more could be achieved.

Social Policy Bonds would enlarge the pool of people with an interest in achieving social and environmental goals. They would inject incentives into all activities currently undertaken to bring about social goals. We looked at this overarching source of efficiency in Chapter 5, but one consequence of it deserves more consideration here: the encouragement a bond regime would give to investigate new activities and experiment with different activities in different regions.

Government has real difficulties in investigating new approaches in its social and environmental programmes. This is partly because government is generally more interested in preventing failure than in rewarding success. In many areas of social and environmental policy it tends to carry out only those activities that it can plausibly justify on the basis of a past record. These activities need not be very efficient, or even partly efficient. As far as many government bodies are concerned they need only to have been tried in the past and not to have been publicly identified as disastrous. This is not a strategy that will optimise performance; nor is it even designed to minimise failure. Rather it is designed to minimise the *public exposure* of failure. It leads to the continuing of inefficient, unimaginative activities, whose main recommendation is that they have been done before. As the persistence of social problems attests, these activities are not always very successful.

Government also finds it more difficult to terminate failed activities than the private sector, partly because government cannot go out of business in the same way as private sector companies, and its employees know this. As John Kay writes:

> The [British] experiment with comprehensive education was a perfectly respectable piece of social and educational engineering which happened to fail. No-one should be criticised for embarking on it. What should be criticised is that the experiment was compulsorily undertaken on a nationwide basis, that there was no process for measuring its consequences (as distinct from the extent of its implementation) that there was great reluctance to acknowledge that it had failed, and that no-one was required to bear any responsibility for what had gone wrong.[101]

Neither can government readily try different approaches in different regions, partly because then it would have to face criticism from people who had experienced the less successful ones. So government typically adopts a uniform approach. In some policy areas, such as education or the environment, it is too easy for central government to override the wishes of local authorities, while local authorities themselves are tempted to override the policies of, say, individual schools or private property owners when it comes to education or environmental matters. But smaller policymaking bodies, be they local government, individual schools or private property owners, often want to employ diverse approaches, and these approaches might well be optimally efficient *in the local circumstances* at achieving desired outcomes.

In one area, for example, crime might be a very obvious and direct result of unemployment. A factory closure might be expected to lead to a soaring crime rate in one particular locality where, perhaps, young males would be put out of work. But under most countries' crime-reduction regimes there is very little incentive for anyone to explore this link and see whether diverting funds from, say, the police to employment creation on a small scale, would be a better way of fighting crime. Most governments would find it politically difficult to subsidise the continued operation of one particular factory when similar factories would receive less favourable treatment simply because their employees were deemed to be less likely to commit crimes if their factories closed. Yet that might be the most efficient way of reducing the crime rate. Another example: screening for certain forms of cancer might be found to be of particular benefit only to women in poorer households. Yet the government would find it politically very difficult to deny such screening to *all* women. In a Social Policy Bond regime, bondholders would put maximisation of their return per unit outlay, which in this case would be maximisation of the health returns from cancer screening to the taxpayers' dollar, above such considerations.

Uniform approaches often go hand-in-hand with government's tendency to enlarge its own role. Government often applies its regulations regardless of whether or not they are appropriate in particular circumstances. Take the costs of complying with burdensome regulations for small businesses. The UK's Care Standards Act of 2000, is just one of many instances. It obliges every care home to have at least 14.1 square metres of private and public space for each elderly resident and at least eight single rooms for every double room. This sort of legislation has meant that over the past five years, at a time when the number of dependent elderly people in the UK has been rising, 50 000 care-home beds have been lost—about ten per cent of the total—and as a result 5000 much-needed hospital beds are occupied by elderly people who do not have acute medical needs.[102] Another example: potential employers can be deterred from starting a business because a government body insists that would-be employees are at risk from, for example, an absence of fire escapes. Government denies people the choice of whether to accept a slightly higher risk of a fatal accident at work in return for a job. While it is all very well to protect workers in this way, when people cannot find work locally they have to travel. In doing so they may well face a risk of dying in a car accident far higher than that of being trapped in a building with no fire escapes. Other examples are even more obviously absurd. The European Union, for instance, insists that abattoirs be tiled. Logic therefore dictated that a snail farmer was told to tile his packing room, which was classed as an abattoir, up to the ceiling to catch the blood.[103]

Social Policy Bonds would encourage investigation of local circumstances, on the basis that doing so could lead to more efficient ways of achieving targeted outcomes than a uniform approach. The most efficient solutions for many social and environmental problems are *not* always known in advance, and the optimal choice is seldom a one-size fits all, top-down, government-dictated policy. More often, they are a matter for investigation and experimentation, and a wide variety of approaches is essential. These will not all be successful and Social Policy Bonds, unlike conventional policy, ensure that approaches that fail or outlive their usefulness are allowed to expire. Bondholders might find, after a bit of experimenting with different approaches, that certain activities work better than others under certain conditions. They would take the best of these approaches, and apply them where their return would be greatest, and they would recognise that, for certain objectives, a mosaic of diverse activities would be most efficient. Under the current regime there are many policies and institutions that outlive their usefulness through institutional inertia or sentimentality.

Similarly, and partly because they frequently opt for uniform approaches, governments often move too slowly to be effective. Social and environmental contexts often change too quickly for government machinery to keep up.

Efficient costing

Many social and environmental objectives are difficult to value. Social Policy Bonds would share with conventional policy instruments the need for policymakers to make some estimate of the value to society of a specified objective. But they have an advantage over most other instruments in that the cost of achieving the targeted outcome would be minimised and capped. And if bondholders fail to perform and the targeted objective remains unachieved, the budgetary cost to the taxpayer would be zero. In maximising the efficiency with which the outcome were achieved, the market for the bonds would be elegantly efficient in conveying information about the cost of achieving objectives and, crucially for policymakers, how this cost varies with time and circumstances.

Take, for example, the objective of lowering some index of water pollution from 50 to 40 units. Assume that a national government issued one million bonds targeting water pollution, each redeemable for $10 once this lower level has been attained. The *maximum* cost to the government of achieving this objective would then be $10 million. But if the bonds, when issued, fetched $5 each, then the market would be saying that it thought it could achieve this objective for just $5 million. It wouldn't say *when* it thought it could achieve that objective, but that could be inferred from market behaviour and the market value of the bonds compared with other financial indicators. But what if the bonds sold for virtually nothing, and the market value of the bonds failed to move from that floor? That would mean that the government had miscalculated: in the market's view there would be no realistic chance of the objective being achieved for an outlay of $10 million in the foreseeable future. The government could respond in different ways:

- It could wait for new technology to arrive, or for circumstances to change in other ways, such that the market would see the objective as becoming more easily achievable, and the value of the bonds would consequently rise. Or,

- It could issue more bonds, with the same specification, also redeemable for $10. It might do this in stages, gauging the market reaction to each new tranche of bonds, which would tell the government the maximum cost of achieving the objective.

Either way, the government could be reasonably sure that it would be getting the best possible deal, expressed as 'reduction in water pollution per unit outlay'. Again, this important benefit was mentioned in Chapter 5, but is worth spelling out in more detail. Valuing the *benefit* of achieving a targeted social or environmental outcome is bound to be an uncertain, and to some extent, subjective task, whichever policy instrument is used. But minimising the *cost* of whatever outcome is targeted is a different matter. A government issuing Social Policy Bonds could determine the maximum cost of achieving the objective because that would simply be the total number of bonds issued multiplied by the redemption value *plus* administration costs *minus* any revenues gained on floating the bonds. And, under a Social Policy Bond regime, it would be the collective wisdom of those in the market for bonds that determines how much the government (that is, taxpayers) would actually pay to achieve the targeted outcome: they will have every incentive to minimise that cost.

But the bond mechanism would not merely minimise the *total* cost of achieving a specified objective. It would also indicate the *marginal* cost of achieving further improvements. Say the one million water pollution reduction bonds were to sell for $5 each. This would tell the government that the present value of the expected maximum cost, including bondholders' profits, of reducing water pollution from 50 to 40 units would be $5 million. The government might then suppose that it could afford to be more ambitious, and aim for a further fall in pollution to 30 units. It could issue a million additional bonds redeemable when this new lower concentration were reached. These would (probably) have an initial market value of less than $5, reflecting the (probably) diminishing returns involved in lowering the nitrate concentration. The point is that, by letting the market do the pricing of the bonds, the government would be getting an informed view of the *marginal* cost of its objectives. So if the bonds targeting the new level of 30 units were to sell for $4 each, then the maximum cost of achieving that objective would be $11 million, being equal to: $5 million (paid out when the level fell from 50 to 40 units) plus $6 million (paid out when the level fell from 40 to 30 units). The marginal cost of a 10-unit drop in water pollution would thus have been revealed to have risen from $5 million to $6 million. Should the government aim for a further fall to 20 units? Following such water pollution-targeting bond issues *it would have robust information about the cost of doing so.*

This is, of course, a simplified example and in fact the bond market would continuously update its pricing information. Say that improvements in technology, of the sort that might be stimulated by an initial issue of bonds targeting water pollution, made it much cheaper for farmers to reduce their water pollution emissions. Bondholders may, for example, have financed successful research into new varieties of grasses that exhibit better uptake of nitrogen fertiliser that would otherwise pollute rivers. How would the market react to such a development? Once the new varieties' effectiveness had been revealed, the value of all the bonds would rise. Instead of being priced at $5 and $4, the two water pollution issues of the example might sell for $8 and $7. The total cost to the government of redeeming these bonds would not change: it would remain at $11 million (though redemption would most probably occur earlier). But the market would be generating new information as to the likely cost of future improvements in water quality. The market would now be expecting reductions of 10 units of water pollution to cost $2 million (from 50 to 40 units), and $3 million (from 40 to 30 units). The new grass varieties would have reduced the costs from $5 million and $6 million (respectively). So the cost of any further pollution reductions would also fall, and by following market price movements policymakers could gauge approximately by how much.

These figures are hypothetical, but they do indicate the role that markets for Social Policy Bonds could play in helping the government, and taxpayers, decide on their spending priorities. The importance of this sort of market information can hardly be exaggerated. The failure in history of central planning can plausibly be attributed to the absence of market-generated information.[104] Market prices reflect all of the information used by all who transact, or choose not to transact, in the market. Central planning fails in comparison with a market economy because it encounters the limits of human beings' calculating capacity: no individual or group of individual planners knows or feasibly can know all the dispersed information that is embodied in prices. Even with a sound incentive system in place—and the centrally planned economies had some fearsome systems—without the information that only markets can generate the computational task of organising an efficient allocation of resources is too great. Prices incorporate and simplify all of the dispersed information implicit in getting a product or service to the marketplace. Markets for Social Policy Bonds would continually generate and reveal this information to policymakers and all those involved in achieving social and environmental outcomes—probably for the first time on a systematic basis. *A Social Policy Bond regime would combine market information with incentives to use it efficiently: the synergies arising could be of enormous benefit to society as a whole.*

Such benefit goes beyond the increase in returns that taxpayers would achieve on their funding of social and environmental programmes. It enlarges the scope of such programmes to include those to which government can hardly put a price. Goals that are critical, but that have not been attempted before—protection against climate change or nuclear terrorism, for example—deny governments a precedent. Because, under the current system, they lend themselves open to abuse by unscrupulous bidders for government contracts, they are in danger of being under-resourced, or not considered at all. A bond regime, though would open up the bidding for achievement of such goals to all, and on a continuous basis, making their targeting a feasible option for the first time.

Stability

A Social Policy Bond regime would help guarantee stability of policy objectives. Bonds could target goals with a necessarily long lead time and bondholders would not be deterred from taking measures to achieve them by fears of a reversal of government policy—or, indeed, a change of government. Only the ends of policies, not the means, would be laid down by government. Obviously the objectives would have to be carefully defined, but there is a wide consensus over what constitutes at least the most basic of our most social goals. A government would be unlikely to repudiate such universally desired *objectives*, even if a ruling party with a different political outlook had issued the associated Social Policy Bonds. The risk that it might (and so become the first government *openly* to support higher unemployment, lower standards of health care, etc) would be not much greater than that of a government refusing to redeem fixed interest stock issued by any of its predecessors. This risk, always present, is factored into the prices of conventional government-issued bonds, and in no way impedes the operation of bond markets.

Importantly, governments would have to give assurances as to their future behaviour if the bonds were to be as successful as possible. For maximum success, they would also have to choose their objectives in consultation with opposition political parties as well as the electorate.

Because Social Policy Bonds could target broad objectives, which are more likely to be stable over time, they would probably have *informational advantages* over more narrowly specified policies. As an example, let us take the myriad ways in which health care funding can be allocated. The government has to make these resource allocation decisions on the basis of data that are necessarily incomplete. How can the government know in detail the effect that spending on, say, cancer diagnostic machinery will have on the overall health of the nation, as compared with subsidising the cost of nicotine chewing gum? So, by default, health expenditure is influenced by groups of medical specialists with little incentive or capacity to see improvements in the *general* health of the nation as an objective. As a result, funding of these specialities depends to a great extent, on spurious factors.

Importantly too, such factors vary over time. A celebrity victim of cancer, say, could divert funding away from more cost-effective health programmes. Similarly, a high-profile, visually gripping, event could undermine rational allocation of resources. For instance, in the aftermath of a tragic rail disaster in London that resulted in the deaths of 40 people the UK Government came under considerable pressure to order the installation of an automatic braking system for trains that go through red signals. Cold calculations showed that this would cost around $21 million for each life that the system could be expected to save. This is around five times the figure that the UK Treasury used as its benchmark valuation of a human life, which means that if the government had succumbed to pressure to install the automatic braking system it would have diverted funds from more cost-effective life-saving projects, and so caused the loss of more lives than it would have saved. A Social Policy Bond regime that had as its objective the maximising of the number of lives saved per government dollar would not waver in the face of one-off events.

Stable objectives would also mean that uncertain scientific relationships need not be proven beyond doubt before work could begin on achieving them. This advantage, and the other advantages that come from long-term stability of policy goals, combine to make Social Policy Bonds a better policy for some large-scale environmental problems, of which climate change is one.

Transparency

Social Policy Bonds would make policy objectives more *transparent*. By focusing on outcomes, rather than activities, they would explicitly identify social objectives. They would encourage indirect, as well as direct, means of achieving them: efficiency would be the overriding criterion. Focusing on identifiable outcomes would encourage constructive participation in the political process, which would mean that measures taken to achieve them would be more likely to attract public support. At least as important, a bond regime would stipulate the maximum value that society wished to place on an outcome. This would have to be decided and made explicit before any bonds could be issued. Costing outcomes in this way would make the tradeoffs between social outcomes more transparent, and make more realistic people's expectations of government. In today's politics, costs of achieving outcomes are obscure, and the language of political debate, at least in the mass media, rarely includes the crucial concept of tradeoffs between different social goals.

Transparency in goal-setting would make virtually impossible two further obstacles on the way to efficient achievement of social goals:

- 'Capture' by bureaucrats: transparency of policy goals would make government unlikely to name itself the beneficiary of its own policies.

- Taxpayers' funding of corporate and middle-class welfare: bonds would make explicit the desired outcomes, and so would make it more difficult for government to launch projects that in effect tax the poor for the benefit of the middle class or the rich.

Transparency means clear and explicit objectives. Consider the European Union's Common Agricultural Policy. Its supposed objectives, as laid down in 1957 in the Treaty of Rome, are:

1. to increase agricultural productivity,

2. to ensure a fair standard of living for [farmers], and

3. to assure the availability of [food] supplies,

4. ...at reasonable prices.[105]

These vague, mutually conflicting and uncosted objectives would not have been acceptable to people formulating desired outcomes for targeting by Social Policy Bonds. A bond regime would force a rethink on other policy issues too. Drugs policy, for instance. Under a bond regime it would be difficult to avoid asking hard questions. Is a reduction in drug taking an end in itself, or a means to an end? If the latter, then what are these ends, and would it not be more efficient and transparent to target them directly? Unemployment may also have to be seen in a new light. Again, is lower unemployment an end in itself? Or a means to an end? Some studies have indeed suggested that the strongest influence on happiness is employment: people with jobs are very much happier than the unemployed.[106] But if lower unemployment were seen mainly as a way of ensuring that fewer people fall below a certain income level; or if it were seen as a means of lowering the crime rate, or improving mental health, then some combination of these objectives should be the targets for government policy.

Under the current outcome-free policymaking system, members of the public can get away with speaking with forked tongues. They can—and do—claim that they want to cut total government spending. But when asked whether they want to see cuts in spending on any specific project (except foreign aid) they are opposed. Most people say they want to see less government regulation in general or are indifferent to current levels. But they then speak out in favour of all *particular* forms of regulation. Similarly with social welfare: one US survey found that 64 per cent believe too much is spent on welfare, but only 26 per cent are willing to actually enforce a two-year limit if welfare recipients would have to take a 'low wage that would make it difficult to support a family'.[107] There is nothing necessarily hypocritical about this. It is an almost inevitable and excusable consequence of a policymaking system that concentrates on everything except costed outcomes. The notion of trade-offs is buried—as far as the public is concerned—beneath an avalanche of confused, vague, mutually conflicting objectives, anecdotes, and attempts to shift blame.

This could not happen under a Social Policy Bond regime. Questions about what people actually want, and the trade-offs involved would be unavoidable *at the outset* of a Social Policy Bond issue: questions that are rarely posed, and still more rarely answered, under the existing policymaking regime.

Even where there is increased pressure for accountability under the existing regime, policies such at the Common Agricultural Policy have a momentum of their own. It is never made transparent of course but for those who manage these policies and their other beneficiaries, any visionary goals were largely forgotten a long time ago, to be replaced by the goal of perpetuating both the policies themselves and the institutions that administer them.

Transparent social goals would require transparent processes for formulating them. And a clear expression of desired social outcomes and their relative priorities would mean that progress toward them could be accurately monitored. Such transparency would also make the sources of any policy errors or deficiencies more identifiable. Perhaps that is one reason why it has rarely been a major feature of government activity over the decades.

Correlation with public benefit

A less obvious benefit of a Social Policy Bond regime would arise from the existence of a means of acquiring wealth whereby private gain would be strongly and inextricably contingent on public benefit. Many bondholders, whether institutions or individuals, would start out rich and, if their bonds rose in value, would become richer. But working successfully to achieve desired social goals would most likely be seen as a laudable way of acquiring wealth. There are intangible benefits from having people or institutions grow rich in this way. There are many disaffected people who, in some cases no doubt justifiably, view with suspicion or alarm the very high incomes or (apparent) profits of corporations engaged in activities of little obvious net social or environmental benefit. They are also unconvinced that 'trickle-down' occurs to any meaningful degree. Wealth, in these people's eyes, is the result of exploitation. Social Policy Bonds would shift this worldview and, by helping people take a more positive view of the act of earning an income and accumulating wealth, could make for a more cohesive society.

7

Practicalities and potential pitfalls of a government-run Social Policy Bond regime

If governments were to issue Social Policy Bonds for large amounts, this would represent a radical change in the way in which our society does things. At first sight, a bond regime may seem outlandish: it would appear to mean government giving up its responsibility for achieving social goals to the private sector. It would also allow private companies to profit from the public purse. But it is important to realise that whoever issues Social Policy Bonds would merely be contracting out the *achievement* of social objectives. A government that issued the bonds would still set these goals and, by undertaking to redeem the bonds, would still be the ultimate source of finance for the projects that achieve them. Moreover, competitors in the market for the bonds would bid away excessive company profits. People would need to be reminded of these facts when asked to contemplate a bond regime. Still, the concept does raise some important questions. Could free riders undermine operation of a bond regime? Could a bond regime generate perverse financial incentives? This chapter begins by looking at these questions, then goes on to consider other practical aspects and potential pitfalls of a Social Policy Bond regime.

The Free Rider question

Many people might purchase Social Policy Bonds with the idea of doing nothing but holding on to them until they could sell them at a profit. Such passive investors would have no intention of doing anything to help achieve the social goal targeted by their bonds. Some of them could be casual purchasers who would buy the bonds with the same intent as they might a lottery ticket. They would hope to hold bonds until their redemption, or until their market value had risen sufficiently high for them to enjoy a worthwhile capital gain. Other passive investors might be speculators who thought that the likelihood of the targeted objective being achieved quickly were greater than the rest of the market believed it to be—in other words, that the bonds were underpriced.

Another category of passive investor might be the hedger. These would be people who, in the absence of the bond issue, would stand to lose if the particular targeted objective were achieved. Hedgers might buy the bonds as a form of insurance against that possibility. If crime were targeted, for example, hedgers might be those who breed guard dogs, for instance, or glaziers who operate where street crime is prevalent. (Actually, though, the losers from particular Social Policy Bond issues might not be clearly identifiable in advance, because the bonds would not stipulate *how* a goal is to be achieved. So, bondholders might decide that one of the most effective ways of reducing crime would be to subsidise the cost of guard dogs to home owners, which would *increase* demand for the animals.)

Casual purchasers and speculators would want to become 'free riders', hoping to benefit from any increase in the bond price without actually participating in any objective-achieving projects. Hedgers wouldn't particularly want the value of their bonds to rise, but their bondholding would similarly reduce the supply of bonds available to active investors. None of these passive purchasers of Social Policy Bonds would do much to help achieve targeted goals. However, markets for the bonds would work to limit the benefits from passive investing. To see this, assume that most of a particular issue of bonds were held by would-be free riders. Then very little, if anything, would be done to help achieve the targeted objective. As the objective became more remote, the value of all the bonds would fall. And as the bonds lost value, they would make a more attractive purchase for people who *were* prepared actively to help achieve the targeted objective. So free riders would be tempted to sell, even at a loss, rather than see the value of their bonds continue to fall. Some history of falling bond prices would tend to make free riding on Social Policy Bonds less appealing with future issues. Free riding then would become a self-cancelling activity. There are other reasons why bondholding would be unattractive to potential free riders:

- Individual free riders would have no incentive to collude with other free riders, because the more they did so, the more remote the targeted objective would become, and the further would the value of their bonds fall. This would act so as to limit any free riding activity to small players.

- As with other financial instruments, small players would have to pay higher transaction costs than the bigger institutions—the ones that would be most likely to initiate objective-achieving projects.

- Small players also would not have access to the research that would enable big players to value the bonds accurately. Therefore they would be at a disadvantage in the market.

Note also that even if free riders were to gain from holding Social Policy Bonds, they would be doing so only because their bonds had risen in value as a result of a targeted objective becoming closer to being achievement. As well, attempted free riding would have positive effects: it would add liquidity to the bond market.

In short, there are grounds to believe that free riding would not seriously undermine the operation of a Social Policy Bond regime, mainly because it is unlikely much free riding would occur, and partly because even if it did occur, it would not impede the operation of the bond mechanism

Perverse incentives

Assume that a national government issues Social Policy Bonds targeting air pollution. Bondholders might then try to persuade or bribe polluting firms to reduce their emissions. But what if polluters spurned bondholders' blandishments and continued to pollute at the same level? Bond prices would therefore fall, and polluters could collude to buy them at a lower price. They would then profit by reducing pollution and redeeming their bonds. If a pattern of such behaviour were established, would not polluters then be the only investors in future issues of bonds targeting pollution? A quick answer would be that the targeted objective would still have been achieved for a sum equal to, or less than, the maximum cost for which the issuers have allowed. True, the cost would be lower if there were no such collusion. But another answer is that bonds are only one weapon in a government's armoury. Regulation of pollution, or the threat of it, would work to raise the market value of the bonds, and make such behaviour risky. This type of behaviour would probably be a threat only when there were a few big polluters who could collude. (In such circumstances a bond regime might anyway not be the best pollution control mechanism, because their informational advantages over tradable permits for example might not be so significant.) But what if, following a bond issue, businesses were to pollute *more* than they otherwise would, and gain from bondholders paying them to stop? In effect they would pollute more on the expectation they would receive enhanced payment for reducing pollution in the future. This behaviour would also, however, have some risk attached, because bondholders might calculate that the most cost-effective reductions could be achieved by businesses other than such anti-social polluters, or that the objective could be achieved in other ways such as, for example, removing air pollutants from the atmosphere. If pollution were a by-product of production, then the output of these polluters would be at an above-optimal quantity, so their pollution increase would not be costless.

But there is still the possibility that cynical, polluting businesses could profit from such behaviour. Or even that people who previously generated no pollution whatsoever might begin to pollute so that they could benefit either from bondholders' paying them to pollute less, or from buying pollution control bonds cheaply, and then reducing their pollution and selling their bonds at a higher price. In all these cases there need be no collusion amongst bondholders. For 'market fundamentalists' contemplating using Social Policy Bonds as the sole means of achieving social and environmental goals, this might constitute a fatal flaw. But, again, the bonds would almost certainly complement a government's regulatory powers—including its powers to make new regulations and charge companies on the basis of how much pollution they emit. In such instances there would probably be enough existing or potential legal (and moral) sanction against cynical polluters to ensure that it need not happen. Governments would certainly retain its powers to tax or regulate in ways that would make perverse increases in pollution more risky, or criminal. And it bears repeating that, in a bond regime, bondholders would have powerful incentives to see that any existing rules against pollution were enforced, or that new and effective regulations on polluters were imposed.

Nevertheless, and more generally, Social Policy Bonds would work by generating financial incentives for people to achieve particular goals and these might encourage people to break the law to do so. Examples of acts that would be illegal, but that certain bond issues might encourage, are:

- emitting pollutants that, while unspecified in bonds targeting pollution, were still controlled or banned;

- forcibly preventing people from registering as unemployed, if bonds targeting unemployment were issued; or

- falsifying data used to compile measures of longevity or infant mortality that were elements of a targeted health objective.

Acts such as these are already illegal and will continue to be so, but before issuing Social Policy Bonds governments should be aware that there would be greater inducements to commit them. Bondholders would need reassurance that government would not relinquish its existing sanctions against illegal activities.

The bonds might also induce people to modify behaviour in ways that, while not illegal, would undermine what they were trying to achieve. So, for example, if bonds targeting the number of reported property crimes were issued, bondholders might lobby insurance companies not to insist on police reports before paying out. Or they might persuade, or pay, insurance companies to raise their excess levels. Either activity would discourage people from reporting minor thefts. Neither would do anything to reduce property crime, but they would each make the targeted objective, lower numbers of *reported* property crimes, more achievable, and so lead to a rise in the bonds' market value. Insurance companies themselves could own the bonds, and so it would be in their own interest to deter people from reporting property crimes. In this particular case, the objective could be more carefully specified so as to target not 'reported crimes' but, for instance, the number of people who, in surveys of the public, say that they have experienced property crimes.

If higher levels of literacy were targeted, bondholders may be tempted to lobby in favour of easier reading tests. Again, judicious specification of the targeted objective would help: the bonds could stipulate the exact reading test to be used, or that the test would have to be certified as appropriate by a specified panel of impartial literacy experts.

In general though, carefully specified objectives might not always eliminate or mitigate the kind of illegal, or negative-but-legal, activities that the bonds may stimulate. So how could this potential problem be solved? There are of course examples, under the existing regime of the successful exploitation of perverse incentives. North Korea, for example, is being offered substantial aid in return for halting its nuclear programme. Egypt receives aid from the United States for not making war on Israel. At the national and local level, compelling examples are harder to find, perhaps because once such cases become known they will encourage unwelcome attention and, possibly, legislation. The same constraints would apply under a bond regime, possibly to a greater extent: in today's political environment policymakers and officials can escape or deflect censure because the adverse results of their policies are difficult to relate to their cause. If Social Policy Bonds were to lead to negative effects, the relationship between these effects and their cause would be easier to identify, and deterring such effects would be simpler than doing so under the current activity- or institution- based funding arrangements. As well, we need to consider closely the role of government in a bond regime, and the way in which the bonds could be introduced.

Introduction of a Social Policy Bond regime

Broad objectives like bringing about climate stability or world peace, would show Social Policy Bonds to their best advantage over conventional policy instruments. The freedom to shift resources into the widest possible range of approaches would generate the biggest benefits over the current regime. But, to be realistic, it is unlikely that any mainstream international organisation or national government will be the first to issue Social Policy Bonds, even when their current policies are manifestly failing. More likely is that the first backers of Social Policy Bonds would be private individuals—see the Annex.

Even if governments follow private individuals in issuing Social Policy Bonds, they are likely to do so cautiously. They could try out the bond principle on an experimental basis at first. Initial goals could be relatively small scale and uncontroversial, and the bonds could complement, rather than replace, existing government or local authority programmes. Amongst the first targeted objectives could be petty crime in particular cities, or the amount of litter deposited on city streets, or illiteracy rates of schoolchildren or adults. Local authorities could also issue bonds that target the water quality in rivers, for instance; indicators of success could be the number and variety of fish present. Unemployment amongst racial minorities, or in particular cities, could also be early targets of a Social Policy Bond regime. Such contained, easily identifiable goals would help the bonds gain acceptability amongst the public, and encourage policymakers to discuss and refine the concept. Watching out for negative behaviour of, or on behalf of, holders of such locally issued bonds would be a fairly simple matter. And if local authorities issued bonds in tranches, targeting incremental improvements in indicators, observing and remedying any negative behaviour would be even simpler. Later tranches of bonds could incorporate provisos stipulating that they would be redeemed only if any unwanted, and previously untargeted, activities did not exceed a minimal level.

Bond issuing authorities would apply lessons learned from such trials to different bond issues, while central government could collate and apply these lessons before issuing bonds with national application. When bonds target new objectives for the first time they would be especially likely to encourage unanticipated negative behaviour by bondholders. Lessons learned from such initial issues could be applied to later issues targeting the same objective. These lessons would extend beyond how to deal with bondholders' behaviour. They might, for instance, give some direction as to the circumstances under which bonds could best be used as complements to existing policies, and when they could safely replace them.

A cautious, gradual, introduction of Social Policy Bonds would be one means of minimising potential problems arising from a bond regime. If, despite such an approach, bondholders behaved illegally, government could prosecute the perpetrators. And if bondholders behaved in negative, but legal ways, government would have other options. In ascending order of severity, government could:

- persuade or cajole bondholders into toeing the line. It could do this publicly or privately—initially, at least, bondholdings could be registered in the same way as shares;

- buy back bonds, which would have the effect of lowering the market price of bonds remaining on the market (by reducing the total redemption funds; see Chapter 5);

- legislate against the negative activity; or

- declare the bonds null and void, and offer compensation related to the bonds' issue price or their current market price.

Effects on government's behaviour

Integration of Social Policy Bonds into the policy-making system could lead to problems arising from government's role as creator of statutes. Government has the power to pass laws that would affect bond prices, or its actions could influence bond prices in other ways. For instance: government could come under great pressure not to increase unemployment benefits from holders of bonds targeting the number of registered unemployed. Note, though, that the source of the pressure, and the motivation for it, would be easy to identify and that lobbying is a perfectly legitimate activity. There is no reason why bondholders, in common with other pressure groups, should not lobby politicians. They would be doing so mainly out of financial self-interest of course. But existing pressure groups are also self-interested, and in the case of bondholders their self-interest would be more likely to coincide with society's interests if targeted objectives were correctly specified. Bondholders would lobby for legislative change, but their reasons for doing so would be transparent.

The role of legislation in improving our social and physical environment should not be understated. 'Market fundamentalists' sometimes attribute social and environmental benefits to market forces alone, while neglecting to mention the role of government regulation in bringing about improvements. Thus Bjorn Lomborg, writing about the much improved air quality in London states that 'for the greater part of the twentieth century [the improvements have] been due to a change in infrastructure and fuel use and only slightly, if at all, connected to environmental worries expressed in concrete policy changes.'[108] He attributes falling particle concentration levels for the European Union and the United States to 'reducing consumption of fossil fuels, especially high-sulfur coal, [to] using smoke scrubbing equipment on power plant smokestacks and [to] increasing energy efficiency'[109] without mentioning the role of regulation in spurring or requiring those changes.[110]

So to holders of Social Policy Bonds, government legislation can be a tool like any other. When they assess the value of the bonds, potential investors would take into account the likelihood of changes in legislation and their potential influence on the speed at which the targeted objective could be achieved. These influences would though make it important for there to be some element of consultation when selecting targeted objectives. People become wealthy by exerting influence on politicians under the current system, but they and their effects on behaviour are not always identifiable. As now, under a bond regime it would be up to politicians to weigh the evidence for and against any course of action promoted by lobbyists, with due regard to the lobbyists' motivation. And it would be up to potential investors in Social Policy Bonds to take into account likely or possible changes in the legislative environment when bidding for the bonds.

The threat of bondholders' lobbying governments for legislative changes could have a positive aspect. For bond issues to be as successful as possible, governments would ideally give assurances as to their future behaviour. These could mean making relatively simple decisions early on. They might, for instance, decide now on the type of reading test to be used to determine literacy in a decade's time. But they could also choose to be more definite about their long-term spending plans. Take bonds targeting national crime rates: would-be bondholders would be very interested to know as much as possible about government's projected expenditures on policing. Similarly, prospective purchasers of bonds targeting atmospheric pollution would want to know, for instance, the government's petrol taxation, electricity generation or road building plans. Government would maximise interest in the bonds by being as open about its legislative and spending intentions as soon as possible. Government could also undertake *not* to do such things as reduce police numbers—such assurances would doubtless be subject to the usual scepticism attending pronouncements of this type.

The question of government behaviour can be seen in a different light. Government, as well as bondholders and society in general, would want Social Policy Bonds to be successful. Its assurances about its legislative and spending plans will never be absolute but, by giving what assurances it could, a government would enhance the market for the bonds and be able to achieve more social goals with the same budget. One way that a government issuing Social Policy Bonds could do this would be for it to specify that, as far as possible, its behaviour would be determined by objective criteria. So government might declare to potential investors in bonds targeting unemployment, for example, that changes in unemployment benefit payments would be strictly related to movements in a specified retail price index.

Of course, if the bonds were to target only small changes in unemployment, or crime rates, or air pollution, or whatever, the government's long-range plans would not be so significant to prospective bondholders. Targeting incremental improvements in social indicators, it might emerge after trials of the bond concept, could be the best way of dealing with the uncertainties of future government behaviour. Alternatively, there may be many social goals for which it turns out that government's behaviour is a relatively insignificant component of the uncertainty that attaches to investment in any financial instrument: markets routinely deal with uncertainty by attaching lower values to riskier instruments.

While government's assurances about its future behaviour would exercise investors' minds, they would also be important to people who are consumers of government services. There would be important implications for bonds that target welfare expenditure. Take for example Social Policy Bonds that, aiming to tackle unemployment, would be redeemed only when spending on unemployment benefit fell by a certain level. Bondholders would then have an incentive to discourage people from applying for, or continuing to receive, unemployment benefit. They might lobby government not to increase the unemployment benefit paid to each person on the unemployment register, or even to reduce it. While it is difficult to imagine bondholders' doing so, and thereby incurring the wrath of much of the rest of society, there are no compelling reasons for making such lobbying illegal. But where government *should* draw the line, firmly, is on the question of who decides whether or not a person qualifies for state benefits. Decisions as to eligibility for state benefits must remain with the state. This is mainly for ethical reasons: these benefits are set, ultimately, by the political process, and are anyway little more than a safety net for most recipients. Bondholders should have the right to provide alternatives to these benefits; even to pay people not to claim them. But they should not have the right to decide who should qualify for them.

Weighting component elements of objectives

There are practical difficulties in weighting the components that make up indicators of certain social and environmental objectives. One component of a 'climate change' objective, as defined in the redemption terms of bonds target-ing climate change, could be 'number of people worldwide killed in adverse climatic events'. There are practical difficulties in defining what counts as an adverse climatic event, and there are boundary issues as to whether a particular death counts as caused by a climatic event or not. But there are also conceptual issues: how would, say, 1000 such deaths be weighted against other compo-nents of a climate change objective? Or, if crime is to be targeted, how many thefts of mobile phones, say, be equivalent to one murder?

There are undoubted conceptual problems here; the important point though is that *exactly the same issues arise in any policymaking environment*. Under the cur-rent system, trade-offs between possible outcomes are not made explicitly, but that does not mean they do not occur. They do, and because they are fudged, they can be made according to arbitrary, undeclared, criteria. Under a Social Policy Bond regime, in contrast, policymakers would be obliged to make explicit their weightings of each component of a targeted outcome. One likely consequence is that, apart from being more stable over time, such elements would be made on a more rational basis. Say that an overall national crime objective is to be targeted, and that it has amongst its components, theft and dangerous driving. How much weight would the street theft of a mobile phone have compared to a conviction for dangerous driving? A Social Policy Bond regime would have to be explicit about such weightings: under the cur-rent system, no such discipline exists.

Assessment of indicators and insider trading

A bond regime would rely on authoritative, accurate and timely monitoring of the targeted social or environmental problem so that progress towards its solu-tion could be impartially assessed. There would probably be private sector information gathering, but the definitive, official, figures would have to be seen to be independent of bondholders, who could benefit unfairly from dubi-ous data collection. Naturally the information as to how close the objective were to being achieved would have value. It would not be difficult, for instance, to imagine the latest official unemployment figures being sought in advance of official publication and used for 'insider trading' of bonds targeting unemployment If too much insider trading went on, it would increase the riskiness of the bonds to those without access to this information and tarnish their value as an investment. So how could it be minimised?

- Those involved in gathering, collating and processing relevant data could be bound by terms deterring or forbidding them from abusing privileged information.

- If large sums of money were at stake, there would be a great deal of private information gathering: investors, bondholders, and financial commentators would take their own soundings throughout the lifetime of each bond issue. There would be more interest in more frequently updated information, so that progress toward achieving objectives could be more readily charted. All this would serve to remove some of the allure from privileged figures that had yet to be publicised.

- Indicators for targeted objectives could be chosen with a view to minimising the possibility of insider trading being an important factor. Some imprecision about how objectives would be measured would help: a government could stipulate that bonds targeting such objectives as urban atmospheric pollution or crime rates in cities would be redeemed on the basis of data from a random sample of cities, rather than from all cities or a predetermined set of cities.

- The objectives themselves could be chosen to minimise the possibility of insider trading. Bonds targeting long-range objectives, such as cutting crime rates or unemployment by 50 per cent rather than 10 per cent, would probably be less sensitive to insider trading. With long-range objectives, each datum illegally withheld from the bond market would probably represent a smaller proportion of the total relevant information available to the bond market, and so have a lesser effect on the bond's market value.

None of these ways of mitigating insider trading would always be fully effective. That said, there are already sensitive indicators, such as unemployment or retail sales figures, that are capable of moving markets, and so there are already in place mechanisms to keep such information secret until it is time for publication. There are also sanctions against those who obtain, and act on, such information illegally. These mechanisms and sanctions might need to be strengthened under a bond regime, but it remains to be seen how important abuse of insider information would be. While insider trading does mean that unscrupulous people benefit at the expense of the public, it does not generally impede the operation of markets. Markets continue to function and the possibility that a low level of insider trading goes on is generally discounted by the broader market.

Futures and options markets

Another possible source of perverse incentives could arise from the development of futures and options markets in Social Policy Bonds. These would enable people to benefit from a falling bond price, so giving them an incentive to delay achievement of the targeted goal.

It is quite likely that there would be futures and options markets for large bond issues, and it is almost certain that the price of any particular Social Policy Bond would not always be increasing along an upward trend from its float price to its redemption value. It would be justifiable, as well as efficient, if bondholders could hedge against consequent falls in the value of their assets. People who do not hold bonds might want to participate in markets for derivatives of bonds, some of which would rise in value as the targeted goal became more remote. This in turn means that speculators and short sellers could certainly profit from *short-term* bond price falls, and the question is whether these people would then take steps to impede progress towards any targeted goal.

There are two main reasons why they would probably not. The first is that, in the long term, the weight of money would be against them. Provided sufficient funds were allocated to achieving the targeted objective, there would be a net positive sum of money payable if the targeted objective were to be achieved, and a net zero sum paid as long as the goal were not achieved. All the long-term incentive would be to achieve the targeted objective. Those who, for whatever reason, would suffer from achievement of the objective could be compensated by bondholders, or bribed to change their ideas. Note also that for every buyer of a 'put' option there would be a seller, and that for every futures contract *bought* on the expectation that the bond price would fall, there would be an equivalent futures contract *sold* on that basis, so that the net incentive generated by derivatives would be in line with the incentive created by the underlying financial instrument, the Social Policy Bond: in the long run, this would favour achievement of the targeted objective.

The other reason that short sellers, or holders of put options, in Social Policy Bonds might not take actions aimed at interfering with achievement of the goal is that such actions might well already be illegal or, again given the incentives that the bonds would generate, be made illegal once the bonds had been issued.

Government as purchaser of government-issued bonds

Government agencies could, as competitive suppliers of objective-achieving services, participate as active investors in Social Policy Bonds under certain conditions. Unlike in industry the private sector would be unlikely to cry 'unfair competition', even if the operations of these agencies were heavily subsidised, because its own bonds would appreciate as a result of the government, or government-inspired, activity.

If government agencies were to participate in the market for government-issued Social Policy Bonds, they should not have privileged access to information. Also, it is important that any profits they receive, or losses that they incur as a result should accrue to that agency. The people who work for government agencies must have the same incentives as private sector bodies to perform efficiently. This would change the character of these agencies, and would probably lead to their ultimate divorce from the public sector.

Government agencies could, of course, buy and sell Social Policy Bonds issued by the private sector, provided they did not abuse any access they have to relevant, privileged information.

Existing institutions and the transition to a Social Policy Bond regime

Few bodies charged with achieving social goals are currently paid in ways that encourage better performance. Nevertheless these bodies are the main sources of expertise for solving social problems and some of them are bound to be efficient, or to be capable of becoming efficient, in doing so. It would be unwise as well as unfair and unnecessary to cut their funding too severely. The answer, at least for goals in policy areas for which there are already significant institutions, would be a gradual transition.

Take health, for example. In the UK, central government provides funding for health authorities (for spending on doctors, hospitals and prescriptions) according mainly to population level, age and need. Government also supplies funds directly to medical research organisations and academic institutions. A transition to an outcome-based, rather than institution- or activity- based, funding programme would see the funds from government gradually decline, while expenditure allocated from holders of Social Policy Bonds to the outcomes that these institutions are collectively trying to achieve—longer life spans and a better quality of life, say—would gradually rise.

On introducing such a bond regime a government could decide to reduce its funding of health authorities and research institutes by 1 per cent a year, in real terms. (The government could allocate the saved funding to the future redemption of the health bonds it has issued.) So after five years, each health authority would be receiving directly from central government only 95 per cent of the funding that it formerly received. But bondholders could choose to supplement the income of some of these health bodies. They may judge a particular group of health authorities to be especially effective at converting the funds they receive into measurable health benefits, as defined by their bonds' redemption terms. Particularly effective health authorities are likely to be working in deprived areas, where small outlays typically bring about larger improvements in health. Or bondholders might judge a particular research body to be worthy of additional funding, because it was conducting excellent research into a condition that would be likely to respond especially effectively, in terms of health outcomes, to additional expenditure. In such cases, bondholders would supplement their selected health authorities' or research institutes' funding. It may well be that these favoured bodies end up receiving considerably more than their former income throughout the lifetime of a bond regime.

It could also happen that investors in bonds targeting health look at completely new ways of achieving health objectives; ways that currently receive no, or very little, funding. To give a not entirely unbelievable example, they may be convinced that one of the best ways of achieving society's health objectives is to deter teenagers from driving. Following this logic, they may find that one of the most efficient ways of doing would be to lay on subsidised taxis for teenagers attending parties in certain areas. It is difficult to imagine how our current activity- or institution- based government fund allocation mechanisms could decide on such a programme. More generally, it is quite likely that holders of bonds targeting health outcomes would greatly expand funding in areas such as health education or preventive medicine that rely on expertise outside those bodies traditionally devoted to health care.[1]

Could bonds targeting remote objectives, such as increasing longevity significantly, or reducing the crime rate by half, be compatible with a gradual transition of the type described above, where funding to existing health institutions reduces by 1 per cent annually? At first sight there would be an apparent mismatch between such incremental reductions in government spending and the time scale needed to reach long-range objectives. The critical point here is that bondholders would be investing not on the basis of the annual reductions in government expenditure on existing health institutions, but on the basis of the redemption value of all the bonds issued. To be more precise, it would be this total redemption value, minus the bonds' existing market value, that would inform bondholders' investment decisions. This sum could be many times each year's incremental reduction in government's institution-based spending. One of the virtues of a Social Policy Bond regime is that *even in the short term bondholders would begin to invest in projects with a long-range objective* on the expectation of capital gains that might arise only in the distant future.

The accumulated reductions in spending to existing institutions would be one, but not the only, factor influencing how much government decides to spend on achieving a specified social goal. Also important would be the financial savings (if any) that achieving the objective would bring about, and the value society would place on any nonfinancial benefits.

---

1.   "We spend vast sums to lengthen the lives of terminally ill patients by a few days and refuse to make modest investments that would prevent millions of needless illnesses and deaths.", Ronald J Glasser, *We are not immune: influenza, SARS, and the collapse of public health*, 'Harper's Magazine', July 2004 (page 38).

Similarly gradual transitions would be warranted in other areas, such as education and crime, where schools and police forces, some of which are bound to be much more effective than others, are well entrenched. These institutions would receive slowly diminishing absolute levels of funding directly from government, while bondholders would again focus their spending on especially rewarding, in terms of specified education and crime outcomes, projects and institutions. As with health, it is likely that those areas that are initially most disadvantaged would again provide bondholders with the greatest return per unit outlay.

In newer policy areas, particularly the environment, it may be possible to expand spending allocated via the bonds at a faster rate: expertise in the environment is still relatively mobile, and it would be easier to quickly establish new outcome-based institutions or to reorientate existing ones.

Interaction with existing programmes and projects

Although changes in the source of funds would be gradual, those involved in existing institutions may well react by quickly reviewing how *all* their existing programmes and projects operate. If bondholders saw existing programmes as being particularly effective in achieving targeted outcomes, then they would be inclined to invest in them. On the one hand, the switch in funding would warn existing institutions that they could expect to see their relatively ineffective operations receive diminishing funds in the future. On the other hand, their effective operations could look forward to higher—possibly much higher—funding. Even a gradual transition involving 1 per cent annual cuts in funds allocated to existing institutions that was balanced by a bond issue could bring about a rapid change in the way existing bodies conducted all their programmes. They may have to devote some of their resources into persuading bondholders of the cost-effectiveness of their activities; but this would not represent a radical difference from the way these bodies lobby for government funding nowadays. Under a bond regime they would have to do their lobbying on a more transparent, outcome-oriented, basis.

Would governments play fair?

Might issuing governments themselves try to avoid redeeming Social Policy Bonds, either by reneging on their commitments to do so, or by doing what they could to stop targeted goals from being achieved? The answer is: probably not. If governments were to issue Social Policy Bonds, they would be doing so as representatives of their citizens. They would therefore be under strong moral pressure to comply with their commitment to supply funds for bond redemption, and not to take actions impeding progress toward the targeted goal. But it would also be in governments' own interest to fulfil their obligations. If they did not, they would be discrediting the entire bond principle, which they might well want to deploy again, either domestically or as participants in efforts to solve global social or environmental problems.

What happens once an objective has been achieved?

When an objective becomes close to achievement, the issuing body could float a new set of Social Policy Bonds aimed at maintaining the achieved outcome or at further improvements. Sustaining the outcome beyond the period specified in the original bond issue would probably be cheaper than achieving it, while further improvements targeted by a second bond issue would most likely cost less, in terms of benefit per unit outlay, than those achieved by the first issue. There are three main reasons for this:

1. Assume that a bond issue aimed at reducing the level of some indicator from x led to its reaching a level of y. Most probably it would take more than a withdrawal of this funding for the indicator to revert back to x. Why? If the indicator represents the rate, in per cent, of unemployment in one area, for example, many of the newly employed would stay in work, even if the absence of further expenditure on a bond issue meant that their salary would revert to the level that had previously failed to attract them into work. This would be partly because they were now more aware of the existence of low-paid work, partly because of the costs and disruption of reverting to an unemployed lifestyle and partly because they would now find the prospect of being unemployed less attractive than previously. If the indicator represented air pollution, to take another example, maintaining lower levels of pollution could be cheaper than achieving it because people would have invested in machinery or other systems that cost less, per unit benefit, to keep running than they did to set up.

2. In a similar fashion, investors in Social Policy Bonds would learn from their experience of achieving the objective targeted by the first bond issue. They would have looked for, and experimented with, dif-

ferent methods of solving the targeted social problem, and would be able to choose the most efficient solutions for subsequent bond issues. If maintaining the cleanliness of a river, for instance, were targeted, then it is likely that any know-how about monitoring systems or equipment installation would be more cheaply available once an initial targeted lower level had already been achieved.

3. Less specifically, it is likely that general improvements in productivity, mainly arising from technology (including information technology), will continue to occur in our economies, and that bondholders would make use of them.

Of course, new issues of Social Policy Bonds might not be the most cost-effective way of maintaining the achieved outcome. There might well be circumstances in which alternative government actions, such as legislation or institutional monitoring, could be preferable.

Conclusion

The introduction of a government-backed Social Policy Bond regime would be accompanied by operational challenges and problems, not all of which can be anticipated. But these potential problems should not be overstated. Existing laws, careful choice and specification of targeted objectives, more transparency in government as to what it wants to achieve and how it will behave would probably circumvent or remedy most of them. And some of the problems that a bond regime would entail are the inevitable result of policies that have, as their measure of success, quantifiable indicators. In an increasingly complex and interlinked world, the trend toward using these indicators for policymaking purposes is likely to continue, regardless of whether Social Policy Bonds are issued or not. The broader point is that the likely performance of a bond regime needs to be compared with the results of current policy-making methods.

8

Application to climate change and violent political conflict

Both climate change and violent political conflict are extremely complex, potentially catastrophic global concerns. The first is recent, the second as old as humanity. This chapter looks in more detail at how the Social Policy Bond principle could be used to address them.

Climate change

Climate Stability Bonds would be issued on the open market and would become redeemable for a fixed sum only when the climate had achieved an agreed and sustained level of stability. In this way there is no need for the targeting mechanism to make assumptions as to *how* to stabilise the world climate: that would be left to bondholders.

Ideally, Climate Stability Bonds would be internationally backed. They could be issued by a world body, perhaps one supervised by the United Nations or World Bank. This body would undertake to redeem the bonds using funds that could be obtained from all countries in proportion to their Gross National Product. It would be up to individual countries to decide how to raise funds, presumably from taxation revenue. Importantly though, the bonds would not be redeemed until the objective of a more stable climate had been achieved. The bonds would be issued by open tender, as at an auction; those who bid the highest price for the limited number of bonds would be successful in buying them. A fixed number of bonds would be issued, each redeemable for, say, $1 million only when climate stability, as certified by objective measurements made by independent scientific bodies, has been achieved. Once issued, the bonds would be freely tradable on the free market.

People will differ in their valuation of the bonds, and their views will change as events occur that make achievement of a stable climate a more or less remote prospect. They will also change as new information about climate, and about the causes of climate change, is discovered.

There are obvious difficulties involved in defining what a stable climate actually is, *but the same difficulties apply when attempting to monitor the success or otherwise of Kyoto.* Presumably scientists will measure the effects of the cuts by monitoring such objectively verifiable indicators as temperature, change in temperature, rate of change of temperature, precipitation, and many others, at a wide range of locations. But it might be agreed that a bond regime should also explicitly target less scientific measures, such as the frequency and severity of adverse climatic events, the numbers of people killed or made homeless by such events or the insurance payouts to which they give rise. Most probably, a Climate Stability Bond regime would target simultaneously a wide array of these variables.

What would bondholders do?

We saw in Chapter 2 that Kyoto is particularly unsuitable for mitigating global climate change, mainly because it does nothing to encourage the exploration of new activities that could offer more climate stability per dollar expenditure. It focuses on one single possible cause, anthropogenic emissions of greenhouse gases, whereas it is almost certainly going to be better to target a wide array of potential causes. (Issuers of Climate Stability Bonds might wish also to devote resources to reducing the *impacts* of climate change—which is not part of Kyoto's remit.)

1 Investigating new activities

The Social Policy Bond principle specifies and rewards outcomes; it does not prejudge how these outcomes shall be achieved. For an objective as broad and complex as climate stability, it is better to encourage a full range of activities than to specify in advance, and with only current scientific knowledge, that it shall be achieved in one particular way. An ideal policy would not discourage research into, and application of, new, more efficient solutions than those that can currently be envisaged by policymakers. A policy such as Kyoto, that seeks to constrain certain prescribed activities and reward other prescribed activities, may not be optimally efficient, because our knowledge of the results of these activities, and of ones yet to be discovered or investigated, is changing all the time.

Climate Stability Bonds are not incompatible with the science underlying Kyoto. If bondholders' incentive-driven research leads them to believe that cutting back greenhouse gas emissions is the most efficient way of achieving climate stability, then that is what they will pursue, but on the basis of cost-effectiveness, rather than through being compelled to comply with a top-down approach that has been dictated by the very limited scientific knowledge that exists today. Cost-effectiveness in carrying out the existing envisaged way of attenuating climate change may be important, but so too is the fact that Climate Stability Bonds would encourage people to investigate new activities that may be better at stabilising the climate, or mitigating the worst effects of climate change.

Many scientists, technologists, engineers and biologists, in countless research bodies the world over, are looking at the causes and effects of climate change and how to deal with or mitigate them. But there is no overall mechanism in place to allocate funding for these bodies on the basis of their likely cost-effectiveness. Within some countries, cost-effectiveness may be one criterion used to allocate funding. But in general, funding for a particular body depends on a range of factors, including ones that have little relevance to efficiency such as the body's existing size or existing level of funding, its contribution to the local economy, its fundraising skills, or the persuasive powers of its public relations directors and their relationship to senior politicians.

Under the current regime, funding for climate change research projects has to compete with demands from a wide range of other government expenditure items. These projects may well be – indeed, most probably, are – run by people with the highest integrity and scientific knowledge, and it is highly likely that *within each body*, funds will be allocated impartially and with a view to obtaining the best result for each dollar outlay. The problem is that there is no overall incentive that will ensure that funds are allocated *between* these bodies, or to the creation of new ones, with a view to *overall* efficiency, defined as reduction in climate instability per dollar outlay.

Kyoto's inefficiencies are likely to be extremely costly. Its climate-stabilising activities were chosen on the basis of science fossilised in the year 2000. Climate Stability Bonds, in contrast, would allocate funding in such a way as to encourage the exploitation of new initiatives. Any resource savings would be potentially of great value to those most in need of government funds, or to the environment generally.

2 Responding to local effects and changing circumstances

The second point, the incentive to experiment with different activities in different regions, is significant in that, while climate change is a global problem, some of its most severe impacts on human life will be local. Unlike Kyoto, Climate Stability Bonds can target these effects, rather than their assumed causes. The bonds could be made redeemable subject to the achievement of such outcomes as reductions in the numbers of people killed or made homeless by climate-related events.

Climate Stability Bonds that incorporate such outcomes into their overall objective would encourage investigation of local circumstances. Here the superiority of Climate Stability Bonds could translate directly into alleviation of human suffering on a significant scale. If the bonds were to target a reduction in the numbers of people killed worldwide by storms then funds for such projects as sea defences, for example, would be allocated under a bond regime to those areas where the most benefit per dollar outlay could be obtained. One result is likely to be that bondholders would invest more heavily in sea defences in densely populated poor countries like Bangladesh, rather than in equally vulnerable, but thinly populated prosperous countries. There is nothing to stop these countries using their own funds for such purposes, but it would seem proper that global funds should be used to maximise the benefit to the world's population.

Similarly, a bond regime is readily adaptable to changing circumstances. An unexpected increase in the frequency of storms, for example, or a rise in the sea level that exceeded all projections would, under a bond regime, lead to a channelling of climate-stabilising funds into alleviating the worst effects of these unanticipated events. Under Kyoto the massive global resources deployed supposedly to stabilise the climate through greenhouse gas emission cutbacks cannot be so responsive.

Efficient costing of objectives

Many environmental objectives are difficult to value, and achieving a higher degree of climate stability is no exception. Climate Stability Bonds share with conventional policy instruments the need for some estimate of the value to society of a specified objective. We saw in Chapter 5 that, unlike Kyoto, a bond regime would cap the *maximum* funding to be spent on achieving climate stability. But Climate Stability Bonds have a further advantage over Kyoto in that competitive bidding combined with tradability guarantees that the *actual* cost of achieving the targeted outcome is also minimised. The market for the bonds would generate important information about the cost of achieving climate stability and, crucially for policymakers, how this cost varies with time and circumstances.

Climate Stability Bonds are efficient not only in supplying climate stabilising services, but also in pricing societies' climate stabilising objective, and for much the same reason: the people who make up markets gather and reveal more information than a handful of government agents, and they have an incentive to use it efficiently. With an objective that is so totally difficult to value, Climate Stability Bonds have an enormous advantage over systems that rely on a handful of 'experts' to attempt to cost. To be frank, though, even that is overly kind to our current resource allocation mechanisms: in fact resources for global long-term projects whose payoff is uncertain are generally unrelated to potential benefits. Governments generally pitch them at the minimum level they can get away with, while trying to satisfy their critics at home and overseas, and Kyoto is no exception. Governments could not so escape their responsibilities under a bond regime.

Transparency

Climate Stability Bonds would help make policy objectives more transparent. Under a Climate Stability Bond regime the combination of targeted outcomes constituting the desired level of climate stability is explicitly identified. There is an important political dimension to this: focusing on a set of identifiable outcomes would encourage constructive participation in the political process.

This means that measures taken to achieve these outcomes will be more likely to attract public participation, understanding and acceptance, if not support, than attempts to cut back on greenhouse gas emissions. At least as important, the maximum value that society wishes to place on its climate stability goals will also have to be decided and publicly known when the bonds are issued and before any programmes have begun. Once that has been determined, the issuing body will be able to decide on the bonds' redemption value and the number of bonds to be issued. Costing outcomes in this way would make the tradeoffs between climate stability and other global goals more transparent.

It is important also that a clear expression of the desired outcome, as embodied in the bonds' redemption conditions, would mean that progress toward it could be accurately monitored.

A stable objective

Achieving and sustaining a significantly higher degree of climate stability is likely to take many years. How is Kyoto likely to fare when more immediate and obvious claims on scarce government or national resources, arise? Or if new science shows Kyoto to be insufficient, inefficient, unnecessary or even counterproductive? Well-chosen climate stability goals are likely to be far more stable than any unproven link between cause and effect, such as that between anthropogenic greenhouse gas emissions and climate change. Decision makers currently see cutting greenhouse gases as the best way of tackling climate change, but there is no necessary reason why this will always be the case. It needs to be said again that there a possibility, and it is a possibility strong enough to discourage whole-hearted participation and compliance with Kyoto, that:

- science will lessen the relative significance of any link between anthropogenic greenhouse gases and climate change,

- new events will deter governments from ensuring their countries' compliance with their Kyoto obligations, or

- new governments will come to power who will assign Kyoto a lesser priority or repudiate it entirely.

Under a Climate Stability Bond regime, the stability of the *desired outcome* makes it unlikely that investors will be deterred from taking measures to achieve it just because of changes of this sort. This contrasts with Kyoto, by whose targets some governments, most notably the US Government, refuse to be bound. Significantly, these governments object not because they disagree with Kyoto's aims, but on the grounds that the proposed mechanisms are inefficient and costly (and unfair in that developing countries are not also obliged to cut their greenhouse gas emissions). Kyoto is vulnerable to changes in either scientific knowledge or political attitudes that would make other governments change their minds, and think along the lines of the current US administration. Under a Climate Stability Bond regime, it would remain the responsibility of bondholders to decide on the most efficient means of achieving the goal. Once the goal had been agreed, the effects of any such governmental vacillation would be felt by the bondholders, via changes in the market price of their bonds. The goal of climate stability would remain unchanged, and it would *always be in bondholders' interests to achieve it.*

More attractive money flows

A further advantage of Climate Stability Bonds is that, in many cases, they will have politically appealing money flows. Kyoto begins with inflicting identifiable losses on certain people and countries in pursuit of its greenhouse gas-controlling objective. The scale of these losses has already led to less than enthusiastic participation by many countries in the Kyoto process. Climate Stability Bonds, however, would reward people for achieving successful outcomes. The other, highly significant, money flow advantage of Climate Stability Bonds is that taxpayers will incur expenditure *only when the targeted improvements in climate stability have actually been achieved.* For this reason, the bonds may attract greater political support than Kyoto, with its enormous, financial (and political) costs, payable in advance, for an outcome whose delivery is remote and uncertain.

What about the market-based mechanisms in Kyoto?

A tradable permit regime specifies the maximum amount of pollutant that can be discharged. It then issues tradable permits to emit amounts of pollutant making up this total. Markets decide the price and allocation of these permits. In the United States, for example, markets for permits to emit acid-rain producing sulphur dioxide have been in operation for several years. Tradable permits are especially useful in allocating unpriced resources, such as the assimilative capacity of the environment, and also for targeting pollutants that have marked thresholds.

Kyoto will embody rules and guidelines for 'market-based mechanisms' that allow participating countries to be flexible in meeting their obligations. The mechanisms include greenhouse gas emissions trading, joint implementation, and the Clean Development Mechanism.

Emissions trading allows a country whose emissions exceed its threshold level to buy credits from a country whose emissions fall below threshold. The trading rules have yet to be established, but it is already clear that carbon dioxide will be the key commodity. One tonne of carbon dioxide emissions (or the equivalent of another of Kyoto's greenhouse gases) will be measured as one tradable emissions allowance. These allowances, which may at some point become government-sanctioned credits, can change hands in a variety of ways. In the developed world, if country A can meet its emissions-reduction target without using up all of its credits, it can sell the remaining pollution rights to country B. In addition, developed nations can earn credits by helping other developed nations lower their emissions. Another provision would allow developed countries to earn credits by working to cut pollution in developing countries. One key idea is to encourage green habits and best industrial practices to spread across borders.

How do Kyoto's market mechanisms measure up against a Climate Stability Bond regime? First, and at the risk of being repetitive, is the important fact that Kyoto's policies have as their objective the cutting back net of anthropogenic emissions of greenhouse gases, rather than achievement of climate stability. So even a highly efficient emissions trading system will be efficient only in achieving that particular, limited, outcome.

Second is that emissions trading schemes require large amounts of information if they are effectively to tackle broad objectives. The United States' tradable permit programme that was designed to reduce sulphur dioxide emissions is successful because it is easy to monitor and enforce. Most of the sulphur dioxide emissions came from just 2000 smokestacks in the American Midwest. But emissions of most greenhouse gases result from many sources and many different processes: carbon dioxide, for example, is emitted by cars and homes, while about 8 per cent of greenhouse gases in the developed countries are emitted by the agriculture sector.[111] Immense quantities of information would be needed to establish, monitor and enforce a comprehensive system of carbon dioxide emission controls using tradable permits to pollute. Similarly with some of the other greenhouse gases. A Climate Stability Bond regime, however (assuming bondholders thought reducing greenhouse gas emissions were an efficient way of tackling climate change), would aim for reduced greenhouse gas emission levels, and let bondholders decide how best to achieve them.

In reducing emissions of some greenhouse gases there may be a role for tradable permits, which can work well with intrinsically large-scale processes. Such processes can be monitored quite easily, because there would be no fear that doing so would lead to offsetting increases in pollution via the setting up of difficult-to-monitor small-scale processes. But most greenhouse gases do not fall into this category.

Third: the role of incentives and self-interest under Kyoto is likely to be less pervasive than under a Climate Stability Bond regime. Under Kyoto, markets will be set up for the tradable emission allowances of all participating countries. Each country will be able, through its dealings with other countries, to organise its emissions and removals activities efficiently, *as a country*. But *within* a country, it is only possible, not certain, that governments will establish a system that injects market incentives into all necessary stages leading to the achievement of the country's greenhouse gas objective. Tradable permits to pollute may be one climate policy instrument, but there is a large portfolio of alternatives from which governments can choose. They include: taxes on emissions, or on carbon or energy use; (non-tradable) permits; the provision, or removal of subsidies; the imposition of technology or performance standards or energy mix requirements; product bans; voluntary agreements; government spending and investment; and support for research and development. In choosing a mix of these policies, and in the implementation of most of them, it is unlikely that efficiency will play a prime role. Each government will have to comply with its international obligations to cut (net) greenhouse gases emissions, but it will have little incentive to do so with maximum efficiency: as in other policy areas, political expediency is likely to influence government behaviour.

A Climate Stability Bond regime, on the other hand, would ensure that efficiency, measured as the increase in climate stability achieved per dollar outlay, operates at every level of aggregation, including within every participating country. As well, bondholders would probably allocate their climate stabilising priorities *between* countries differently than will Kyoto. Again, efficiency would be their guiding principle.

Fourth: while the details of Kyoto's emissions trading system have yet to be devised, it is likely that they too will embody the scientific relationships known or assumed at the time of formulation. Kyoto in general suffers from uncertainties over the relative contributions that greenhouse gases make to climate change. A market-based system allowing sinks to offset greenhouse gas emissions would suffer from the even greater uncertainties in the relationships between these sinks and atmospheric greenhouse gas levels. It is likely that any trading scheme would fix these relationships according to today's science: so, for example, a given area of a particular type of forest would be regarded as equivalent to emissions of a fixed level of carbon dioxide equivalent, regardless of any new knowledge that will come to light about the relationships of forests to climate change.

A Climate Stability Bond regime would begin with the same uncertainties, but bondholders would have a powerful and *continuing* incentive to investigate the constantly changing relationships between all these activities, and to *adapt to new knowledge*, always with a view to achieving the goal of a more stable climate as efficiently as possible.

Climate change summary

Climate change is an extremely complex problem. Kyoto's targeting of anthropogenic greenhouse gas emissions is going to involve large numbers of governments, industrialists, economists and technologists. Under a bond regime, a much wider of solutions could be deployed, and market forces would ensure that all participants would have maximum incentives to achieve society's climate stability goals as cost-effectively as possible. Indeed, the identity of these participants would be constantly changing, reflecting our rapidly expanding knowledge about climate change, and its causes and impacts. All efforts would be subordinated to dealing with what is probably our greatest environmental challenge. We should demand no less.

Conflict Reduction

If climate change is our gravest environmental threat, then violent political conflict—war, civil war and terrorism—is potentially our most serious social concern. It is as complex as climate change and already proven to be as devastating in its consequences. How would a bond regime tackle it?

For centuries, idealists and ideologues, politicians, philosophers and spiritual leaders have tried and failed to end war. Most civilians, most governments and most non-governmental organisations would like nothing more than to see a permanent end to war. Yet violent political conflict—war, civil war, and terrorism—continues to destroy hundreds of thousands of lives every year. There are too many in positions of power or influence who are half-hearted about peace; others who feel threatened by it, and others who, for whatever reason, actively promote violence. It is time to recognise that we are not going to solve the problem of war without incentives comparable to those that encourage all too many people to keep conflict going.

So we need a way of promoting peace that can modify or circumvent these people's uncooperative or obstructive behaviour. We need to mobilise the interests of the far greater number of people who want peace. We need to find a way that can co-opt or subsidise those people in positions of authority and power who want to help, and at the same time distract, depose or otherwise undermine those opposed to our goal. Given the failure of innumerable thinkers, statespeople and others from all walks of life, we should look to enlarge the pool of potential peace-builders. We need to harness the resource-allocation power of market forces—after all it is these market incentives stimulate the manufacture and distribution of the weapons, and the scramble for resources, that cause so much human suffering.

Governments, non-governmental organisations, international bodies or individuals who are serious about reducing violent political conflict could back and issue Conflict Reduction Bonds. These would be sold by auction, and redeemed for a fixed sum only when the number of people killed, injured or made homeless by violent political conflict reached a very low level. Bondholders would gain most by ensuring that peace is achieved quickly.

What to target?

The precise definition of the targeted peace objective not merely a technical issue: it is crucial to how Conflict Reduction Bonds would operate. The incentives that the bonds put in place would encourage people to strive to achieve the components that make up the targeted objective, so it is worth looking in some detail at the desirable and feasible objectives of possible Conflict Reduction Bond regimes.

Key criteria are that components of a targeted conflict-reduction objective should:

1. Represent, when targeted, ends in themselves, or be strongly and inextricably correlated to such ends, and

2. Be as easy as possible to measure objectively, reliably and accurately.

The bonds could target an index comprising a wide range of indicators of conflict and peace simultaneously, over the entire world.

Conflict Reduction Bonds could be issued for different continents or regions, with different targeted definitions of peace to suit local conditions. For instance, bonds targeting peace in the Middle East could readily target numerical indicators of dead and injured, as these figures are well documented in comparison to other conflicts. In regions where casualty numbers are unreliable other indicators would have to be targeted. These could include quality of life indicators, such as literacy, or the numbers of people moving across certain boundaries, or the value of weapons purchased by potential participants in conflict. Or conflict-related deaths could be estimated through demographic analyses of census data before and after conflicts, or through indirect mortality measurements such as survey questions on survival of siblings, parents, or spouses. When appropriate, targets could be specified on the basis of random sampling of populations, using such components as 'proportion of interviewees who have lost one family member to violence', rather than unreliable aggregate casualty figures.

Conflict Reduction Bonds could also aim to achieve peace for specified periods: they could be redeemed once the targeted peace objective had been sustained for a period of five or ten years, say.

Possible elements for targeting

Each conflict will have different characteristics, not least in how accurately measures of its effects can be quantified. Particular indicators might be more suited to certain conflicts, but a bond regime could also target global or regional conflict. Below are some possible starting points for compiling components to be targeted by Conflict Reduction Bonds.

• Number of people killed in armed conflicts

Historically even the more basic questions about conflict, such as the identity of the combatants, when fighting began and ended and, more particularly, how many were killed, have been remarkably hard to pin down. Wars merged and split, or had no clear beginning or end.[112] Data on more recent conflicts, including internal conflicts, is still scanty, and different methodologies can produce different results. While armed forces and guerrillas usually know approximately how many people they have lost, they frequently understate the numbers killed on their own side and overstate the numbers killed on the opposing side. Civilian casualties are even harder to pin down. In most conflicts there is no agency charged with counting them, and what figures can be found are clouded in uncertainty, imprecision and confusion. Most casualties of war today are civilians, but estimates of the proportion vary considerably. Globally, it is harder to measure the numbers indirectly killed by conflict, through such consequences of conflict as flight, destruction of infrastructure, or disruption of the economy. But for particular conflicts it may be possible to estimate sufficiently reliable figures.

• Expenditure on armaments

This has the advantage that it is strongly correlated with benefits forgone; that is, it represents the quantity of goods and services that could otherwise have benefited people. Thus, for example, the US and Soviet Union's very large expenditure on nuclear weapons and delivery systems during the Cold War did not translate into direct battle casualties. In the narrow terms of avoiding nuclear conflict, then, the Cold War can be said to have been successful.[113] But the expenditure on nuclear weaponry represents a large diversion of resources away from more valuable sectors of the countries' economies. Nor was it certain throughout the Cold War that conflict *would* be avoided, so there was a high price paid in personal anxiety and fear by large numbers of people in both countries and beyond. And, while the former superpowers have reduced their nuclear weapons arsenals, they continue to hold a huge number of nuclear strategic offensive weapons, which could readily destroy Russian or American society. The decommissioning of nuclear material on both sides has generated environmental concerns.

It might also have accelerated proliferation. An ideal measure of conflict for a bond regime that targeted large-scale, or even worldwide, conflict levels should probably encompass not only expenditure on weapons, but also their distribution. India, Pakistan, Israel and North Korea can be regarded as already nuclear. Iran is believed to be moving rapidly toward acquiring nuclear weapons, while Libya and Syria might also be moving in that direction.[114] The western world has been surprised in the past by the speed at which countries have developed nuclear weapons.[115] Even more frighteningly, weapons of mass destruction are becoming available to private syndicates of all kinds that are not within the jurisdiction of the United Nations, or any other body. The possibility of nuclear proliferation gaining further ground and jeopardizing regional and global stability is very real. And nuclear delivery systems, as well as chemical and biological weapons have also proliferated.

So there is a strong case for including, as components of a bond issue aimed at reducing worldwide conflict, both spending on weaponry in general and some quantifiable measure of proliferation of weapons of mass destruction in particular.

If a range of conflicts is being targeted by a single bond issue, national expenditures could be weighted on a Purchasing Power Parity basis, to approximate the true value of the benefits forgone, and the greater threat posed by similar dollar expenditures on weapons have in areas where they cost less. For example, the same sum spent on smalls arms in African conflict areas could be weighted more heavily than if it were spent on routine maintenance of sophisticated western defence systems. Unfortunately, some components of military expenditures are often treated as state secrets. As well, defence industry structures are very often highly concentrated, or nationalized, making it difficult to obtain data or even good price estimates for military equipment.[116] Nor is there a complete authoritative record of global military expenditure.[117] But for particular conflicts, or potential conflicts, military spending could be one useful component of a conflict-reduction objective.

- Military strength

Military strength is an estimate of both military personnel and military equipment. The rationale for including this measure is similar to that for including military expenditure: it represents both the opportunity cost of resources lost to the life-enhancing parts of the world economy, and it is an indicator also of the potential for violence, and so an indicator of human insecurity or anxiety. While estimates of materiel could be subject to the same imprecision as spending on armaments, numbers of military personnel might be easier to quantify for targeting purposes in some regions of actual or potential conflict.

- Nuclear explosion

The detonation of a nuclear device could be worth targeting in its own right. A nuclear explosion would be easy to monitor and would not only lead, in all probability, to large numbers of dead, wounded and sick, but would represent the breach of a significant threshold.

- Mass media indicators of impending conflict

Conflict Reduction Bonds could also target events that are likely to lead to war, such as efforts to gain public support. There appears to be strong evidence that the underlying intentions of governments can be accurately gauged by a systematic analysis of opinion-leading articles in the mass media, regardless of the relative openness of the media in question. Such analysis allows the prediction of both the likelihood of conflict and what form of conflict—military, diplomatic or economic—will occur.[118] This sort of indicator could be useful as a target where military conflict has not begun, but appears possible, and where other data are scarce.

Discussion

Whether these, or other, indicators should be made the explicit target of Conflict Reduction Bonds depends on the intentions of the bonds' backers.

Take the Cold War, during which the US and Soviet Union spent vast sums on their nuclear weaponry, none of which was actually deployed. Should Conflict Reduction Bonds aim to reduce such spending? Or should we take the view that, since direct armed conflict between the two protagonists did not actually occur, then the sums spent on nuclear weapons would not have made sensible targets for a bond regime launched in the Cold War's early years? There are sound arguments on both sides. Certainly, the expenditure represented not only direct non-military benefits forgone by both economies (and indirect benefits, arising from lower exports, for example, forgone by other economies), but the *potential* for devastating conflict. For both reasons, it would make sense to allocate it some weight as an indicator in a bond issue addressing a broad, worldwide definition of conflict. On the other hand, where less devastating military conflict is actually occurring or is a strong possibility, it might make more sense to attach more weight to such targets as battle or civilian casualties, rather than an expenditure indicator that might anyway be more difficult to calculate accurately.

One danger to be borne in mind when selecting targets, or combinations of targets, for a bond issue, is the possibility that a bond issue targeting one component of a particular conflict might encourage behaviour that aggravates other, untargeted, conflicts or components of conflict. A bond regime focussing on region A, for example, divert conflict-reduction resources away from region B. Or focusing on, say, numbers of armed personnel could encourage a government or military faction to switch spending away from recruitment and into arms purchases. As an ideal, objectives that if not pursued jointly could conflict, should be targeted by a single bond issue. But in most circumstances this would not be necessary, particularly in relation to actual or potential conflicts in which weapons of mass destruction are not an issue. It is quite likely, for example, that if numbers of personnel were reduced, then arms purchases would reduce too, or the capacity of existing materiel to inflict casualties would fall in parallel. As well, provided a bond regime targeted such obvious and meaningful outcomes as reduced numbers of people killed in conflict, it is unlikely that leaving out other indicators like military expenditure would actually cause these indicators to move in a negative direction. These indicators, in general, are correlated sufficiently strongly with the obvious targets to be safely left untargeted. The same can probably be said of the effects of conflict on a region's physical or social infrastructure, or the damage done to the physical environment.

What about United Nations missions, or other undertakings that involve the use of arms for, supposedly, peacekeeping purposes, or for pre-empting larger conflicts? Should the casualties of such 'beneficial' military interventions be included in total casualties to be targeted by a bond regime? Since the aim of these military missions is generally to reduce actual or potential military conflict, then it would be consistent to include the results of casualties they cause in any bond issue that encompasses the region within which they occur: the bonds would then encourage 'beneficial' military interventions insofar as they were successful in reducing the total number of long-term casualties in the region.

As a long-term ideal, a single issue of Conflict Reduction Bonds could target the effects of conflict worldwide, with each negative effect being weighted according to its lethality. Such a bond issue would encourage optimal alloca-tion of the world's conflict-reduction resources. It would thus be theoretically superior to, but perhaps less feasible than, bond issues with more localised objectives. In fact, people are already making efforts to calibrate warfare events and their impacts on societies, and these efforts could form the basis of a future target for bonds. One example is the ten-point scale used by the Center for Systemic Peace.[119] The numbers on this scale represent a categorical indi-cator of the destructive impact of each violent episode on the directly-affected society, similar to that used to gauge the destructive potential of storms and earthquakes. The scale ranges from 1 (low damage and limited scope) to 10 (total destruction). On this scale, the Rwandan genocide of 1994 rates a 7, the ethnic war in Kosovo is rated 4, and the US and UK air campaign against Iraq in 1998–1999 rates a 1. Magnitude scores reflect the widest range of warfare's consequences to both short-term and long-term societal well-being, including direct and indirect deaths and injuries; sexual and economic predation; popu-lation dislocations; damage to cooperative social enterprises and networks; diminished environmental quality, general health, and quality of life; destruc-tion of capital infrastructure; diversion of scarce resources; and loss of capacity, confidence, and future potential. The magnitude scores are considered to be consistently assigned across episodes and types of warfare and for all societies directly affected by the violence. Work is also being carried out into a Human Insecurity Index, based on indicators such as the number of deaths from armed conflict, the incidence of criminal violence and refugee numbers.[120]

The results of these works-in-progress could form the basis of a worldwide Conflict Reduction Bond issue. Targeting reliable indices of the impact of conflict on human welfare, would encourage the impartial allocation of soci-ety's scarce conflict-reduction resources into whichever conflict-reducing activity would do the most good, anywhere in the world, regardless of the prejudices and preoccupations of politicians or the media.

But while aggregate indices could be helpful in targeting global conflict, it is certainly not worth waiting for broad, rigorous measures to be defined and compiled before attempting to reduce particular conflicts. Such measures as 'number of people killed', or 'military spending', can be estimated reliably enough to correlate with human welfare. There is also a strong case for issuing bonds that reward a long period of nuclear peace. As well, a bond regime need not operate in a vacuum. While it could target quantifiable outcomes such as the number of people killed in a conflict, other measures could be in force at the same time as a bond regime. For example, there could be treaty obligations to limit the number and type of weapons deployed, or numbers of armed personnel. The bond concept, fortunately, is a versatile one, and could be adapted to changing circumstances, or evolving views about which elements of conflict are best suited for targeting.

All such elements should, for bond redemption purposes, be measured by accredited impartial bodies. It is likely that there will always be some uncertainty and subjectivity about some of the targeted goals, such as the number of people killed or made homeless by conflict. Accordingly, for a large, government-backed Conflict Reduction Bond issue, the body that verifies and promulgates the measurements of whichever goals are targeted will have to be impartial, trusted, and beyond reproach. Smaller initiatives, though, undertaken by groups of private individuals, could target indicators as reported in the mass media.

Conflict Reduction Bonds would work by building a coalition of interests with a strong incentive to reduce deadly violence as effectively and efficiently as possible.

Their main advantage over existing peace-building initiatives would be their efficiency, but this overlaps with other advantages, including transparency and stability of the policy objective.

Efficiency

Efficiency gains, expressed as the reduction in violent political conflict worldwide per dollar spent, would arise from several linked sources.

Self-interest and market forces would channel conflict-reducing resources into achieving the desired *outcome* efficiently. This contrasts with the current system under which funding is generally allocated to organisations that may be well-meaning, but that are not rewarded in ways that correlate with their success in reducing conflict. A coalition of bondholders would have more freedom to initiate projects that governments and others in positions of power cannot support, or do not wish to support, or *do not wish to be seen* to support. Holders of Conflict Reduction Bonds would have incentives to support whichever conflict-reducing initiatives would be most effective. Their objective and that of the people who would back the bonds would therefore be *exactly the same*. The more efficient were bondholders in reducing the level of violence, the more they would gain from appreciation in the value of their bonds. This efficiency would maximise the reduction in violence that could be achieved per dollar outlay.

The lower the targeted level of violence, the more likely bondholders would be to undertake projects that would pay off only in the long term, but note that it would be unsatisfactory to achieve a low level of violence just for a short period. The ultimate objective is a sustained low level of violence, and that is the targeted objective that would have to be achieved before Conflict Reduction Bonds should be redeemed.

Of course, many enlightened individuals and organisations are already carrying out valuable peace-enhancing activities. But under a Conflict Reduction Bond regime many more might be enticed to do so, while others who hostile to peace could be encouraged to moderate their opposition to conflict reduction measures. Importantly, under a bond regime, funds for building peace could bypass corrupt people in authority or inefficient governments or, by appealing to these people's financial self-interest (if they were bondholders, or bribed by bondholders) could effectively modify their behaviour in favour of achieving the targeted peace objective.

Many world conflicts occur within or between developing countries. Unfortunately, even more than in the rich countries, the stated objectives of politicians and governments differ from their real intentions. In many developing countries powerful politicians use their own hidden networks of placemen in key positions in important ministries to frustrate whatever projects or policies they find inconvenient. Outsiders, including especially overseas aid donors, find little correlation between what the governments in these countries say they want and what they actually want. World Bank and International Monetary Fund personnel officially judge countries on their stated policies and plans, but in many countries these bear little relationship to the way the country is actually run.[121] So it is important that ways of reducing conflict can circumvent any obstructions put in their path by such governments, and Conflict Reduction Bonds would encourage that.

It would be in the interests of bondholders and those whom they influence to seek out those ways of achieving the targeted reduction of conflict that would give them the best return on their outlay. But this would also be in the interests of those, whether taxpayers or private individuals, who would be the ultimate source of funds used to redeem the bonds. Crucially, it would be only when the violence had fallen to the targeted lower level and been sustained for the stipulated period that the bond backers would end up paying for these efforts. Until then it would be up to bondholders to finance those initiatives that they believed would bring about reductions in the violence. Again, this contrasts with the current system, in which taxpayers incur costs for funding conflict-reduction schemes regardless of whether they are effective or not. The body that issues Conflict Reduction Bonds would, in effect, be contracting out the achievement of peace to the private sector. It would still, though, stipulate the definition of conflict that it wanted to see reduced and, by undertaking to redeem the bonds, would still be the ultimate source of finance for that reduction.

Bondholders would be in a better position than governments to undertake a range of peace-building initiatives. Take the Arab-Israeli conflict as an example. Bondholders could conceivably finance sports matches between opposing sides, promote anti-war programmes on TV, or set up exchange schemes for students of the opposing sides. They might even subsidise intermarriage between members of the opposing communities, or try to influence the financial supporters of conflict outside the region to redirect their funding into more edifying activities. They could offer the Palestinians and the citizens of neighbouring Arab countries different forms of aid, including education and scientific aid, and measures aimed at enlightening Arab citizens.

Bondholders could lobby, or work with, the Israeli and Arab governments to, say, give a higher priority to peace studies in schools, but they could also develop peace-teaching projects of their own. While immediate peace might not result, much more could be done to enhance the prospect of *peace in the future*. Bondholders could, for instance, make strenuous efforts in Israel and the neighbouring countries to have some mixed classes of Jewish and Palestinian children at kindergarten and school. Both groups must have the chance of spending time with each other. At the very least there should be opportunities for the younger people from both sides of the conflict to meet, discuss, argue and form friendships.

Other examples of activities that bondholders could undertake would be:

- Lobbying for the elimination of all state-sponsored anti-Israeli and anti-Jewish propaganda, in textbooks, radio, TV, newspapers and the internet; especially in Syria, Lebanon, Egypt and Jordan.

- Promoting exchanges between Israel and its neighbours at all levels, to discuss matters of regional importance including: water resources, the environment, economic integration etc. Any agreed outcomes from such talks could be seen as a bonus: bureaucrats talking to each other may or may not achieve very much, but their talking in itself implies a recognition of the humanity of the other side, which would make armed conflict less likely.

- Lobbying western countries, including Israel, to give Arab countries preferential trade access to the Israeli market. Doing so would give everyone in the region the chance of economic growth and a better life for their children. It would give them a chance to build trust and take a stake in a peaceful future—a chance that the current Arab governments are largely denying their own people.

- Promoting opportunities for the populations of these countries to learn English (and even, eventually, Hebrew).

- Promoting genuine democracy in, and foreign direct investment into, the Arab countries.

The rationale for these last measures is again to give the populations of these countries something to hope for other than the destruction of Israel. More positively, it is to open the eyes of the younger people in the Arab countries to the virtues and rewards of democracy and economic growth. If it works for older people too, so much the better; if not, these measures may at least distract them from the current conflict.

These are only examples, of course, though they do illustrate the potential for peace-building initiatives that are largely ignored by those with influence today. In reality, bondholders would be likely to undertake a range of initiatives, *the precise nature of which need not be known in advance*. It would be up to bondholders to decide on those programmes that would give them the best return for each dollar they spend, and this means they would look for and put into action ways of achieving peace that they believe will be most effective.

They have more latitude than most of those bodies currently involved in conflict-reduction. Governments have real difficulties in investigating new approaches to social problems. As with many social programmes, government is subject to constraints on its behaviour that can limit its effectiveness. Actions such as subsidising intermarriage between potentially hostile factions would arise intense ire, and could be explosively controversial, if undertaken by a national government or by an inter-governmental body such as the United Nations. But they would be less controversial if undertaken by bondholders. If we assume that bonds specifically targeting long-term peace in the Arab-Israeli conflict are issued, then the only question bondholders need ask themselves about subsidising intermarriage between Palestinian Arabs and Israeli Jews is whether it would be cost-effective as a peace-building measure.

Governments' reluctance to explore new approaches to many social problems arises not only from the controversy that a particular new approach might generate, but also because government is generally more interested in preventing failure than in rewarding success. In the almost total absence of a self-evaluative culture[122] it leads to the continuing of inefficient, unimaginative and failed activities.

Another source of efficiency arises from the greater freedom holders of Conflict Reduction Bonds would have to ignore the priorities of the media. Conflict in the Middle East, for example, has a very high media profile—itself a possible inflammatory influence. Conflict in Africa, on the other hand, rarely makes the news. The long-lasting conflicts in Sudan have led to the deaths of at least two million people, the displacement of millions more and a continuing (in mid 2004) desperate humanitarian situation in the south of the country. The death toll in the five years since Congo's civil war began in 1998 is put at between 3.1 million and 4.7 million.[123] These wars rarely feature in the western media. The result is that a disproportionate share of the world's meagre conflict-reducing resources flow to the Middle East, while the wars and civil wars of Africa, which have devastated the lives of millions, receive comparatively little attention. Holders of bonds aimed at minimising conflict over the entire world would allocate resources impartially, giving most attention to reducing those conflicts that, in their judgement, would maximise the conflict reduction that could be achieved per dollar outlay.

International bodies, and inter-governmental agencies share other unfortunate characteristics with national governments. They tend to adopt uniform approaches to similar problems, and they are slow to respond appropriately to rapidly changing circumstances. These deficiencies are apparently inherent in bureaucracies and result from their being no incentives to come up with more diverse or more adaptive solutions to social problems. They have probably contributed to the persistence of social problems in the rich countries, despite the ever-increasing expenditure allocated to their solution. And they can have the same effect internationally. Unlike government employees, however, holders of Conflict Reduction Bonds would have incentives to react to different conflicts in different ways, and to respond quickly and appropriately to events. They would also have incentives to monitor, improve and evaluate these diverse responses and they would have powerful incentives to discard the least promising of their approaches and to follow only those that had been successful and cost-effective in reducing conflict.

Under a Conflict Reduction Bond regime, if bondholders were unexpectedly efficient or if external events were unexpectedly helpful, they could sell their bonds and realise their capital gains. But if bondholders were inefficient, or external events were unexpectedly unhelpful, so that bondholders failed to achieve the conflict-reduction target then *they* would be the losers, not the backers of the bonds. If the bonds were backed by various countries' governments, the ultimate beneficiaries of this feature of Conflict Reduction Bonds would be the taxpayers of contributing countries who, in a departure from the current system, would not have to pay for ineffective conflict-reduction projects.

Efficiency would also arise from the way in which markets for Conflict Reduction Bonds would continuously reveal information, as described in Chapter 6. This would tell the bonds' backers and anyone who might want to supply conflict-reduction services: (1) how close a targeted objective were to being achieved; (2) the potential rewards from buying the bonds and participating in objective-achieving projects; and (3) the likely costs of marginal improvements beyond those already targeted.

Stability

A further advantage of Conflict Reduction Bonds would be the stability of their objectives. Many conflict-reduction programmes will have a necessarily long lead time, and bondholders should not be deterred from initiating them by fears of a change of policy. Under a bond regime only the ends of policy, not the means, would be specified. Current efforts to reduce conflict often depend on particular people or governments remaining in power. Or their success depends on how accurate are particular views about the causes of a conflict, or the nature of the protagonists. As events and circumstances change, these conflict-reduction efforts are often slow to adapt. But under a Conflict Reduction Bond regime bondholders would be free to choose what they believe will be the best ways of achieving peace as cost-effectively as possible. The goal of reduced conflict is more stable over time than the best ways of achieving it. So the bonds would lead to the responsive allocation of conflict-reduction resources. Bondholders would maximise their returns by refusing to overestimate the importance of high-profile, short-term events. Motivated by profit, they would undertake activities that might bring peace only in the long term. These could include such unglamorous and slow-to-act projects as investment in education or in efforts made to end hate propaganda directed at children. There are people and organisations involved in these activities nowadays, but under a Conflict Reduction Bond regime it is likely that their efforts would receive more funding. Stability of the policy objective, reduced conflict, would give bondholders more confidence to invest for the long term.

Transparency

Another significant advantage of Conflict Reduction Bonds would be their *transparency*. The objectives of each bond issue would be clear and explicit. Their over-arching aim would be to achieve sustained minimal levels of a particular conflict (or of conflict worldwide). The bonds' redemption terms would thus make clear to everybody exactly what are the real objectives of those governments, NGOs, and individuals that back the bonds.

Some powerful people in governments, militant organisations or religious institutions would resent the targeting of such objectives by external agencies in this way. But, while under the current system they can oppose peace in ways that attract support, under a Conflict Reduction Bond regime they would have to openly declare their opposition to peace itself. It is precisely this clear focus on the *outcome* of peace—rather than activities, policies, programmes or institutions—that would help mobilise and motivate the coalition working to achieve it.

By focusing on transparent outcomes, rather than activities, Conflict Reduction Bonds would encourage indirect, as well as direct, means of achieving them: efficiency in conflict-reduction would be the overriding criterion for choosing whether to fund an activity. This could bring about changes in the way organisations operate. An aid organisation, instead of focusing solely on, say, the number of households newly supplied with water, would also consider the potential of its activities to reduce conflict. Under a bond regime, it would divert resources into water-supplying initiatives that contributed more to conflict reduction and away from than those that in its view would do little to reduce conflict, or could even aggravate it.

Conclusion

In discussing the scourges of war, civil war, and terrorism, it would seem irresponsible to advocate radical new measures. Unfortunately, despite the heroic actions taken by many individuals, aid organisations and other bodies, violent political conflict is very much a feature of our world today. Man's inhumanity to man seems to be paralleled only by man's ingenuity in fulfilling humankind's unceasing demands for a constant supply of daily necessities and stimulating new demands for an ever-expanding range of nonessentials. This ingenuity results from desires, common to most of us, to enrich ourselves and those close to us. The same ingenuity can and should be used to address our global concerns. If that means a societal shift in resources away from the proliferation of new confectionary or laundry products and in favour of a stable climate and a more peaceful world, most would be prepared to make that trade. It would be irresponsible, indeed, not to do so. There should be a role for market forces, properly channelled, to solve our most serious problems as well as our most trivial.

9

Government and markets: comparison of Social Policy Bonds with other 'more-market' approaches

Many countries' governments have recognised the inadequacies of the conventional approach to solving social problems. Recognising that the market is better at allocating scarce resources than government, they have made various efforts to give the market more influence over these decisions. This chapter looks at some of these alternatives, and contrasts them with government-backed Social Policy Bonds.

Privatisation

Privatisation is the selling of assets owned by government suppliers of services and the transfer of control to shareholders. It has been widespread. In many countries utilities, such as railways, electricity companies and telecoms have been fully privatised. In the UK most of the local authorities' housing stock has been sold to ex-tenants.

How successful has privatisation been? In those countries with rule of law and secure property rights it has had some success, at least when compared to the performance of nationalised industries. There have been some improvements in efficiency, and because of the taxes they pay on their profits, privatised com-

panies now make positive contributions to government funds—a dramatic
change from when they were publicly owned and were mostly a drain on public funds. But some of the labour the industries shed on privatisation has not
found alternative employment, and it appears that it was government's disengagement from day-to-day operating decisions, rather than the transfer of
ownership, that secured privatisation's efficiency gains.[124] Customers have on
balance gained from privatisation, but not hugely. There have been significant
improvements in service to customers where businesses have faced competition, as in telecoms and airlines. Fears that privatisation would lead to a loss of
universal service or to higher charges for the poor have proved unfounded,[125]
but again, regulatory policy has probably been an important factor. Privatisation, according to another view, has apparently created a need for very detailed
public regulation of privatised industries, and this has been quite at odds with
what was expected by the government and its advisors. What we have now 'is
not a clear case of the state withdrawing as an economic agent but rather
changing its role as such.'[126] This might be one reason why, despite widespread privatisation, the volume of government spending has hardly fallen in
the industrialised countries.

Privatisation of services like basic education, health care, and social insurance
would probably not be politically acceptable in many countries; at least, not
without further extensive regulation. The problem is that private businesses
have private goals, and while these may coincide with social goals some or
even most of the time, there will always be some people who either through
their own, or their parents', misfortune, indolence or apathy, will not be well
served by private institutions pursuing purely private goals. This, of course, is
true of the current system, but the current system can claim that because it is
not private it has the public interest at heart. (It may be failing to look after
the public interest, and it may be very expensive and inefficient, but it can
make that claim.) A fully privatised school system, for instance, would have no
market incentive to raise the educational standards of the less bright children
of poor parents.

In short, privatisation can be helpful as one way of giving more meaningful
incentives for people to run services currently run by government agents. But
private companies are not generally rewarded for achieving desirable social
outcomes. Privatisation is merely a transfer of assets, or a disengagement of
government from running certain activities or supplying certain outputs. By

itself, it cannot supplant the government's role as a safety net for the neediest members of society or as a provider of public goods.

Voucher schemes

Education voucher schemes have been used by several states in the north-eastern US, and in the UK. Parents are given vouchers that they can use to purchase schooling for their children from whichever schools they wish, whether they be government or private.

Vouchers assign greater importance to the demands that consumers actually make of an education system, rather than to the services that government employees or others think they should want. Most parents agree on the importance of basic academic subjects. They expect that, at a minimum, their children will have mastered reading, writing, and elementary maths by the time they are out primary school. Parents are also concerned about career preparation. But beyond these basics, priorities differ widely. Vouchers allow parents to make their own decisions, and encourage schools to compete to supply what parents want.

Voucher schemes have some of the advantages of Social Policy Bonds: through markets parents are motivated to seek the best education available at the price, and schools are motivated to supply it. Under a voucher scheme government continues to pay for education. But vouchers do have some disadvantages. Some of these stem from the fact that the vouchers do not specify outcomes. They specify only that they must be used to pay for children's going to school. This works well for those children whose parents are capable of making informed choices, and who are willing to do so. It might not work so well for the children of less informed or less motivated parents, so it would still be possible for desired social outcomes, such as universal literacy, say, not to be achieved. Another concern is that vouchers could encourage the negative aspects of competitive behaviour. Under a Social Policy Bond regime rewards from self-interest would be inextricably tied to outcomes. In voucher schemes, on the other hand, self-interest could take the form of suppliers competing against each other in ways that undermine their ability to achieve targeted outcomes efficiently. This is especially likely when consumers lack information, as is likely to be the case in, say, provision of health services.

As well, voucher systems could not readily be applied to goals that have a strong public good element such as better law and order, improved health care, and better environmental protection. These concerns would make it difficult to apply voucher schemes widely.

Contracting out of existing services and the UK's Private Finance Initiative

Central and local governments have contracted out services previously done by the public sector: in some US states, allocation of welfare benefits has been so contracted out; while in the UK, hospital laundries, and various other services previously supplied by local authorities have been similarly put out to tender. When compared to Social Policy Bonds, contracting out has other disadvantages. Take the UK Government's Private Finance Initiative (PFI), which aims to encourage the private sector to invest in major public infrastructure projects, such as hospitals, schools, and roads. Under the PFI, building projects that would previously have relied on public money are financed by the private sector. Government specifies the outputs it requires, in terms of the nature and level of service required, and invites the private sector to bid for the contract to supply these outputs. Taking hospitals, for example, the private sector partner is usually responsible for:

- designing the facilities according to National Health Service (NHS) specifications;

- building the facilities to time and at a fixed cost;

- financing the capital cost: the private sector partner recovers this cost by renting the facilities to the NHS, generally for periods of more than 25 years; and

- operating the facilities: most of the staff, including cleaners, catering, porters, security and maintenance staff, are employed by the private contractor. Receptionists, secretaries and lab technicians may also be employed by the private sector (but doctors and nurses are employed by the NHS).

When using the PFI the UK Government is, in effect, contracting out the building of the hospital and non-health staffing to the private sector. It is the private sector PFI partner that assumes the risks in each of these areas; this reduces the overall risks to the public sector associated with procuring new assets. Moreover, because the PFI partner's capital is at risk, it will have a strong incentive to continue to perform efficiently throughout the life of the contract.

The PFI, as with contracting out of services generally, is efficient at supplying carefully specified outputs. Specification of these outputs can be a costly exercise (though costs will fall as different public sector bodies share their output-specification experiences), as is the monitoring of compliance, but allowing the private sector to bid to supply outputs is generally more efficient than paying directly from public funds. A report commissioned by the UK Treasury puts the average estimated saving for a sample of projects as 17 per cent.[127] Nevertheless, because it is only outputs that are specified under the PFI, and because of the degree to which they must be specified to ensure efficiency, the PFI, as with contracting out of services generally tends:

- to be limited to particular stages of an outcome-delivering enterprise; and

- to reinforce established ways of doing things.

Outputs, however efficiently supplied, do not necessarily lead to more favourable, or more efficiently supplied, outcomes. So under the PFI a new hospital may be more likely to be built on time, to exact specification, and cost-effectively. But a Social Policy Bond targeting general health indicators would not assume that building a new hospital were the best way of achieving society's health goals in the first place.

Tradeable contracts

What if public sector contracts were made tradeable, so that the winner of a tendered contract could sell the right to supply the service? Perhaps the successful bidding company would have done what it could to achieve a targeted objective, and done so efficiently and quickly. So the value of the contract would have risen, and being tradeable, could be sold at a profit. The new contractor would then still have an incentive to perform efficiently. Tradeable contracts would be similar to Social Policy Bonds, as long as the terms of the contract stipulated that a specified outcome be achieved, rather than an output be supplied. A contract's tradability would help avoid the problem of possible collusion (tacit or not) between bidders for contracts; under the current system, inflated bids can succeed if the bidders agree (explicitly or not) to inflate their bids.

Tradability of contracts would encourage suppliers of services to continue to minimise costs and maintain efficiency *after* they have started helping achieve the targeted goal. Under the current system there may be a tendency for contractors, or their employees, having won a contract, not to maximise the speed and efficiency with which they go about solving the targeted problem or, more likely, supplying the agreed output. While contractors can sometimes benefit from being efficient, they cannot always enjoy this benefit in terms of immediate cash capital gains. There is scope for incentive payments, or penalty clauses, but these are crude, ad hoc arrangements that are costly to administer or impose. Under a Social Policy Bond regime, if bondholders were unexpectedly efficient (or if external events were unexpectedly helpful) they could sell their bonds and realise their capital gains before all the necessary work had been carried out. And if bondholders were inefficient, *they* would be the losers, not taxpayers. The same benefit, in principle, would apply to tradeable contracts to achieve an outcome.

Tradability would also transfer the risk of breach of contract from the tax- or rate- payer to bondholders. If, under a contract system, the successful bidders fail to do what they were legally obliged to do, then it is up to the aggrieved party—the central or local government agency—to take proceedings against them. Even if such actions are successful, they can be protracted and costly. Under a tradeable contract or Social Policy Bond regime, underperforming investors would find a ready market for their contract or bonds in people who believe they can be more efficient.

The main difference between a tradeable contract to deliver an outcome, and a Social Policy Bond issue, would be that Social Policy Bonds could be bought and held by anybody, not just people already involved in carrying out the target-achieving projects, or well set up to do so. So the number of possible bidders would not be limited to a few likely operators, but would be open to all who are prepared to do, or to finance the doing of, things that would help achieve the targeted objective. The fact that anybody could be involved in the bidding for bonds at any stage would discourage people from making excessive bids, so ensuring that social objectives would be achieved as cost-effectively as possible. Compared with tradeable contracts, this would make ownership of Social Policy Bonds more fluid, which would mean more market liquidity, more transparency and an enhanced ability for the government to fine tune its priorities after the outcome has been specified and the bonds issued.

If the Social Policy Bond concept were to generate more market activity, it would make more practical the targeting of remote objectives; ones that may take years or decades to achieve. Many businesses would be reluctant to take on these goals without the possibility that they could benefit in the shorter run. Social Policy Bonds would allow them to do what they could to achieve the target, then benefit from selling their bonds at a higher price, letting the new bondholders continue the advance toward the goal. Similarly, a liquid market for the bonds would make it more quickly apparent that those charged with achieving a social goal had underestimated their costs, or overestimated their efficiency. Under a regime of tradable contracts for which there were no liquid market, such deficiencies might take a fatally long time to become obvious. But under a Social Policy Bond regime the market prices of the relevant bonds would fall, making it clear to everyone that the current contractors were inefficient, and making it easier for other investors to take hold of the reins and pursue the targeted objective. And, as we saw in Chapter 8, there are other advantages arising from the information that the bonds' market prices would generate. To recap: markets in the bonds would continuously reveal information that would tell the issuers, and anyone who might want to supply objective-achieving services: (1) how close a targeted objective were to being achieved; (2) the potential rewards from buying the bonds and participating in objective-achieving projects; and (3) the likely costs of marginal improvements beyond those already targeted.

Summary: Social Policy Bonds compared with other 'more market' approaches

The *contracting out* of existing services suffers because of the need for government to specify in detail what is required. This deficiency also affected the New Zealand state sector reforms, discussed elsewhere. It limits their application considerably and adds to their implementation costs. Similarly, as we saw in the previous chapter, the information demands of tradable pollution permits mean that they can be used only for inherently large-scale processes that can be monitored quite easily.

One aspect of the UK's Private Finance Initiative that is particularly noteworthy is the private sector's willingness to bear the risks of overruns on such items as construction cost. Indeed, this transfer of risk to the private sector is estimated to account for 60 per cent of the forecast savings that result from the

PFI.[128] The private sector's willingness to bear risk, and the savings that result, would bode well for a Social Policy Bond regime, under which investors in the bonds would bear all the risks of achieving outcomes. Because the market would determine the bonds' prices, the cost of assuming all risks would be fair to bondholders as well as the taxpayer.

Because of the limitations inherent in the contracting out of services, it would seem that *privatisation* and *vouchers* are the most widely applicable of the 'more market' alternatives available to government. A combination of privatised schools, for example, and vouchers, could do much to raise standards in education with unchanged, or even reduced, public expenditure. But note the problem of children whose parents have no ability to make an informed decision as to the schooling, or who have no interest in doing so. For education, this could turn out to be a minor problem—at least as compared with that generated by state systems—as the standards of all schools would probably rise in a privatised system. But lack of information would be marked in health care, where most consumers have little idea as to the treatment they need. They rely on the medical profession to tell them.

In general, when a system allows private interests to flourish, there will be some people who suffer either because they are poor, or because they themselves are, or are dependants of, uninformed consumers. Giving the poor purchasing power would help them, but only insofar as they can make an informed decision and are willing to do so. When the service is one like education, most people would probably fall into that category, but not all. And when the service is one like health care, where most consumers are in the dark, the number of uninformed or misinformed people would be very large.

Social Policy Bonds would solve this information problem in ways that privatisation or voucher schemes, or combinations of the two, cannot. They would give a voice to, and focus directly on, *society's* concerns, expressed in terms of explicit desired outcomes. Compared to privatisation or voucher schemes, they would have advantages in education where some people's children may fall through the cracks, and they would have more significant advantages in health care, where most people are uninformed. There are important public good aspects in having an educated and healthy population. But where Social Policy Bonds score heavily over other more-market mechanisms would be in the delivery of those objectives that have an even purer public character, such as reduced crime rates or a cleaner environment.

For the same reasons, a bond regime might also have political advantages. Most of the arguments in favour of continued government intervention in areas like health, education, and welfare crystallise around what would happen to the poor or unfortunate if government were to withdraw. Social Policy Bonds may be superior to other 'more market' approaches, in that government would not relinquish its role in bringing about better outcomes for the poorest members of society. It would simply withdraw from *achieving* these goals, but continue to set these goals, and to be the ultimate source of finance for their achievement. Society's goals are not the same as an aggregation of all its members' individual goals weighted by purchasing power. As a society, there are outcomes like safer neighbourhoods, lower infant mortality, or 100 per cent literacy, which people collectively might want to achieve, and know they can achieve, but which a fully privatised system would not guarantee. Social Policy Bonds, because of their focus on outcomes, would allow full discussion and consultation as to what society's goals are, and how much society values their achievement.

Indeed, public interest in outcomes as against process and institutions might stimulate enthusiasm for serious initiatives currently thought to be beyond the scope of government, including those such as climate change and violent political conflict. The moves towards markets outlined above are a little disappointing: they have meant a bit more efficiency here, a different set of players there, but there has been a marked absence of governments', national or local, harnessing market forces to achieve bold new goals. Perhaps much of the motivation for privatisation and contracting out of services has been to reduce the power of public sector labour organisations. Regardless, we remain in the unedifying position of having the market's efficiencies and incentives being deployed almost exclusively in the service of private sector goals. You are more likely to become rich by marketing a new brand of breakfast cereal in the United States than by doing something positive to raise literacy at home or reduce the incidence of civil war overseas. Social Policy Bonds aim to change that.

10

Objectives for a government-run Social Policy Bond regime

*What sets us against one another is
not our aims—they all come to the same
thing—but our methods, which are the
fruits of our varied reasoning.*

Saint-Exupery; Sand and Stars (1939)

This chapter looks at the criteria for those targeted outcomes that would best be served by a Social Policy Bond regime run by national governments or supra-national bodies such as the United Nations. These are not the only bodies with an interest in social and environmental goals. Private individuals could back their own bond issues with the aim of achieving their own goals, or of supplementing existing efforts by government agents: such bond issues are discussed in the Annex.

But national governments and the international organisations that they finance are still the biggest spenders on social and environmental activities. The question posed in this chapter is: for which outcomes would Social Policy Bonds have most advantages over existing policy? Any set of targeted outcomes will be a matter for discussion, negotiation and constant refinement, but we can identify four criteria that outcomes should satisfy if they are to be best targeted by a bond regime.

1 Broad objectives

In our discussion above, and particularly with reference to climate change and violent political conflict, we touched on the need to tackle broad problems, whose solution would help solve and clarify many other problems. For such over-arching problems, a bond regime would have other benefits in comparison with existing policy measures, which have as their focus activities and existing institutions. Social Policy Bonds would encourage the freer allocation of resources between different policy approaches, and between different regions or even, for global problems, different countries and continents. The benefits of a bond regime would be most marked where there is greater scope for such resource shifts. So, for example, it would be preferable (as we pointed out in Chapter 5) to target an index of air pollution rather than the level of one particular pollutant in the atmosphere. It would be even better to target the general health of the population.

This is the line taken by the US Public Health Service, which began to apply outcome-setting principles to public health as early as 1979, when it set the first national health goals.[129] The three goals of its most recent strategic plan are similarly broad:

- Increase the span of healthy life for all Americans,

- Reduce health disparities among Americans, and

- Achieve access to preventive services for all Americans.

Under a bond regime it would be up to investors in the bonds to identify sub-objectives. Government and its agencies would concentrate on defining measures and monitoring progress toward achievement of its objectives. The private sector, given unambiguous, stable outcomes to aim for, would do what it does best: allocate resources to achieve these outcomes, as cost-effectively as it can.

2 Reliable numerical measure inextricably linked with social welfare

Governments' unequivocal successes have been in achieving positive changes in such indicators as infant mortality and basic literacy and numeracy rates. These figures do correlate strongly with society's well-being, and a prime criterion for outcomes that can be effectively targeted by Social Policy Bonds—and by government in general—are that *when measured, they should be inextricably correlated with improved social welfare.* This applies to all government bodies, whether targeting global, national or local problems. Any targeted outcome must either be an end in itself, or closely correlated to an end.

This would screen out some obviously flawed targets or indicators. Take, for example, the length of hospital waiting lists for certain surgical operations—we all know that waiting *time* is more important. Focusing on single narrow indicators also lends itself to abuse and manipulation (see box).

From 'Letters to the Editor', *The Times*, London, 14 August 1999:

Yesterday I was told by my doctor that she cannot, at present, refer patients suffering from varicose veins for hospital treatment. Today I read your report that hospital waiting lists have come down. Is this coincidence? Are patients with complaints which, while not life-threatening are extremely irritating and debilitating, being denied treatment so that the Government can maintain that it has fulfilled an election pledge?

Equally dubious are such targets as smaller class sizes, or reduced traffic congestion—these are means to unspecified ends, not ends in themselves. But a bond regime would also it would also bring into question larger so-called objectives, such as an 'improved transport infrastructure'. Is that an end in itself, or a means to an end? And if a means, shouldn't we target more directly that which we actually want to achieve? We should at least be asking such questions.

Even more critically, a bond regime would oblige national governments to consider what is in danger of becoming their *de facto* overarching target by default. This is economic growth, generally expressed as rate of growth of

Gross Domestic Product per capita. But amongst other failings GDP does not take into account changes in the quality of the environment, nor the distribution of income. It ignores human capital (the education and skills that are embodied in the work force) and leisure time, and it overlooks such social problems as crime and homelessness. GDP's flaws as an indicator of social welfare are perhaps *implicit in the very act of using quantifiable measures* or any objective criteria to represent our well-being because, above quite low levels of material wealth, our well-being is inescapably subjective, and cannot be a function of a set of numerical indicators.

The mistake has been for governments to take measures that were valid indicators of success in the past—such as fast GDP growth, spending on health or education, rising asset prices, or incomes of public servants or farmers—and continue to target them as such when they have ceased reliably to track welfare. Policymakers sometimes find it hard to shift their priorities, and often end up targeting outdated indicators without regard for whether doing so brings about a genuine improvement in social welfare or not. In the rich countries, the policies that would bring about large benefits for a disadvantaged population were clearer in previous centuries than they are today. Basic health, education and housing programmes were set up by enlightened governments—sometimes against determined opposition—and few would now argue that provision of such services should be left solely to the market to put in place. But the economies of the rich countries are today far more complex, and relationships between cause (government-financed activity) and effect (well-being of citizens) are far less clear.

By refocusing on today's priorities it is likely that governments in the rich countries that issue Social Policy Bonds would target their efforts more on helping the poor and disadvantaged. This is something they claim to do be doing nowadays: tackling poverty and the consequences of poverty is a large part of government's declared rationale for supplying health, education, housing, and welfare services as well as most of its transfer payments. It also implicitly underpins much government intervention in infrastructure, industry and agriculture; though 'strategic' arguments are often also deployed in those contexts. But their poverty objectives are very often conflict with their multiplicity of other objectives, or are targeted only indirectly and implicitly. A bond regime, in contrast, would target poverty directly and explicitly.

3 Complex, uncertain relationships

It is with complex, uncertain relationships that a bond regime might also show large advantages over current policy. Such complexities make it difficult to be sure in advance which policy approaches are going to be most helpful—or will remain helpful when our knowledge about the relationships between cause and effect is continuously changing, as is our ability to alter these relationships. The most characteristic features of our economies – their extended distances and time lags between separating production and consumption, and between governors and governed – aggravate the difficulties of tracing problems to their cause. Even in less sophisticated economies, policies driven by formula or ideology can be unhelpful.[130]

Moreover, there is little incentive in the current system for anyone to track and exploit the effects that policy activities and what can be a very large number of other variables, have on social and environmental outcomes. Typically such relationships are of interest only to government employees, the academic community and, occasionally, the media. While their degree of motivation might be intense at the individual level, collectively they certainly bring less ingenuity to bear than would a much larger pool of potential investors in Social Policy Bonds.

4 Existing policies are ineffective

A fourth criterion is that existing policies have failed, are failing or are expensive and wasteful.

Meeting the criteria

In the nature of things there must only be a small number of objectives that satisfy all these criteria, but they will be important. Climate change and violent political conflict and, in this author's view, ideal candidates for targeting by bond regimes. Eradication of poverty is another, partly because the poor are most in need of government intervention, and also because it is at lower levels of real income and wealth that the correlation between a quantifiable indicator and social welfare is strong and therefore useful to policymakers.[131] A bond regime targeting broad objectives, such as poverty, would divert resources to where they could do most good: that is, where the maximum benefit per dollar outlay could be achieved, and it is those who are most disadvantaged who would benefit from channelling of funds in this way.

Goals that would help the poor and disadvantaged in the rich countries are:

- Improved basic education,
- Lower unemployment, and
- Better physical health.

More difficult to quantify, and less explicitly focused on the disadvantaged, is a lower crime rate. More controversial still would be indicators of mental health. Many of the ills of our way of living find expression in mental illness. But there are formidable obstacles to quantifying any but the most serious mental disorders in ways reliable enough to be useful for Social Policy Bond purposes.

Social Policy Bonds would focus government intentions more successfully than the current system. They would be aimed at helping the poorest and most disadvantaged members of society. They would certainly not get side-tracked, or corrupted, into supporting the better-off or big business *at the expense* of the poor.

It is possible that a bond regime's efficiency gains would mean that some outcomes, currently assigned a low priority because they are expensive, will become more feasible, and so given a higher priority. As well, a bond regime might have to target new threats, especially those arising from new environmental challenges, or improved knowledge about existing threats.

Limitations

'Anything that exists, exists in some quantity,
and can therefore be measured'

—Lord Kelvin

Lord Kelvin's remark is nonsense, of course. An individual's happiness, or its aggregate counterpart for society as a whole, *cannot* be summed up by any conceivable array of quantifiable measures. Some things simply cannot be measured, and policymakers whether in government or not, and whether they issue Social Policy Bonds or not, have to exercise their judgement about them.

That said, measurement of well-being is an expanding area of study, with obvious implications for a bond regime, which could conceivably target such measures directly. In the past, the height of people in poor countries correlated very closely with well-being but data on heights is becoming less valuable as an indicator because improved living standards will cease to affect heights.[132] The Physical Quality of Life Index, or the Anthropometric Index, may fulfil a similar role in the future, but we are still a long way from single measures that measure the overall well-being of large societies. So outcomes such as reduced violent political conflict and better basic education and health will have to do for now.

If numerical indicators are limited, so too is financial self-interest as a motivating force. People perform valuable social or environmental services not only for monetary gain, but also because they enjoy doing them for their own sake, or because they believe them to be the morally right things to do, or because they believe that their actions will advance some cause to which they are committed. These are 'intrinsic' motives, as distinct from external, monetary incentives. Under some circumstances offering monetary rewards can 'crowd out' these less mercenary and more civic-minded motivations or even undermine them. Bruno Frey, a Swiss economist, has researched and written about this effect.[133] Crowding out internal motivation can occur, he writes, because, monetary incentives can undermine people's feelings of self-determination and self-esteem. Also, when external incentives are supplied, the 'person acting on the basis of his or her intrinsic motivation is deprived of the chance to exhibit this intrinsic motivation to other persons.' Not mentioned by Frey, but also plausible is that financial incentives can undermine the cognitive outlook that sees socially and environmentally beneficial services as worthwhile in their own right, rather than as a cost for which compensation and payments must be paid by taxpayers.[134]

While these considerations would have implications for a bond regime, they apply to some degree to existing policy methods. But as Frey says, crowding-out effects are not always significant. In markets that are based on relations amongst essentially self-interested strangers, financial incentives as exhibited through the price effect do work as classical economics predicts. That is, they work to increase supply. And when (as they would be under a bond regime) external rewards are seen as recognition of the importance of, say, civic duty rather than an attempt to 'buy' one's civic performance, they may well support, rather than undermine, moral and other intrinsic motivations.[135] A bond regime could give bondholders incentives to further Frey's research, exploring the relationships between financial incentives and supply of civic performance. They could use this knowledge to minimise the costs of achieving targeted objectives by, for example, finding out when monetary incentives are least likely to supplant the intrinsic motivations of people who help achieve objectives, and concentrating their use in those circumstances.

Alternatives to financial incentives: a note on the Japanese model

The Social Policy Bond mechanism relies on people's responding positively to financial incentives, but are there sources of motivation?

In the right context, social rewards for achievement of economic and political objectives can be as effective as cash. Robert Locke argues persuasively in relation to Japanese society that 'what people are pursuing in the workplace is not so much money as the respect of the people around them…. [The Japanese] have understood that a large part of what money-seeking individuals really want is just to spend that money on purchasing social respect, through status display or whatever, so it is far more efficient to allocate respect directly.'[136]

Rather than offer financial rewards, we could, as the Japanese do, reward people with higher social status. An honours system could go some way toward rewarding people who forgo financial fortune for the good of society. Indeed, many countries have honours systems that are—or were—intended to do this. People also gain status merely by being admitted to exclusive societies, by working for a reputable organisation, or are pleased simply to be recognised in their role by cognoscenti. And many social reformers are quite happy to toil away without needing their efforts validated by any external body. They might be happier for knowing that they are helping to improve the society in which they live but, for a very large number, their reward lies simply in knowing that they are making a contribution.

Whether for good or ill, the context within which social status is barely corre-lated with financial status is rapidly disappearing from many rich countries: social status is becoming more and more congruent with high levels of wealth and income. Our honours systems, instead of compensating people for the financial sacrifices they have made for the public good, are more and more fol-lowing the trend, making awards to entertainers and sportspeople who, what-ever their other troubles, are not financially impoverished. There are still fields of activity, in the academic and religious worlds, for instance, wherein social status and monetary reward do not always go hand-in-hand, but they are shrinking. Re-instatement of a popular culture that confers high status on those who achieve social and environmental goals would be a difficult task in our highly mobile world. It would have to be an evolutionary process. But some progress could be made—not least by those motivated by a bond regime's financial incentives—by aiming to weaken or convert those people whose respect comes from their *anti*-social behaviour; for example, terrorists and other ideological fanatics.

11

The future

Presented as the solution to the complex social and environmental problems that we face, the Social Policy Bond concept could easily be dismissed as a simplistic non-solution. But Social Policy Bonds are not a solution: they are a meta-solution. They are a means of encouraging people to come up with solutions to clearly articulated problems. In this a bond regime is similar to the private market system, which has brought about an immensely improved standard of living for many millions of people. That is also a meta-solution, a system that works by rewarding people for providing goods and services that people want to buy. A Social Policy Bond regime would similarly give scope to enterprise and pluralism to supply solutions to society's problems.

Social Policy Bonds would focus government on outcomes. They would blur the distinction between the public and policymakers. People would take more of an interest in politics, encouraged by the direct link between policy and outcomes. There would be less ambiguity and less ideology. No longer would politicians be able to claim that simply by increasing the amount of taxation revenue that they spend on, say, health, they were addressing society's health care concerns. No longer would the public be able to get away with saying they support mutually conflicting objectives, such as tax cuts, and increased spending. Or 'less regulation' in general, but more regulation for particular industries. Or cuts in spending on welfare, but no cuts on particular welfare programmes.[137]

Social Policy Bonds would give people a more realistic expectation of what their taxes can achieve. Ordinary people could participate more actively and constructively in a regime focused on outcomes than they can today, when the link between funding and outcomes is too obscure to engage the public.

Intra-country comparisons, already compiled in many countries, would take on new significance. People in one city or region seeing, for example, that the level of basic educational achievement of their children was lower than in other districts, might vote for more of their local taxes to reduce that disparity. They would not be discouraged by the fact that they were not educational experts; nor would they look to central government or educational professionals for the answer. Their focus would be on the priority they give to the educational goal as against other social goals.

At the national level, the most obscene wastes of taxpayers' money would disappear. Transfers and subsidies would be delivered to people on the basis of objective measures of need, rather than political influence. People would be given income support because they satisfied some objective criteria showing that they were poor; not because they had deceived the public or played on its emotions. Corporate bodies that benefit from the wide array of disguised subsidies, transfers and import barriers, would lose out, at least in the short term. Instead funds would be devoted to redeeming Social Policy Bonds that reward efficient, effective attempts to achieve genuine social goals.

At the global level where we are confronted by urgent, daunting challenges, our institutional structures are even less adapted to facing them than are most national governments. In the long run the widespread acceptance that self-interest can be channelled into solving social problems could have far-reaching implications. International transfers of taxpayer funds appear to be at least as prone to misallocation as their domestic equivalents. International or global social or environmental problems such as climate change, war, or infectious diseases could be made the targets of future Social Policy Bonds. Corrupt governments could be major purchasers of such bonds. Or they could be paid by major bondholders to alter their policies. Either way, they would have incentives to modify their behaviour to help achieve these desired outcomes, whether these include ensuring that food supplies reach their own starving citizens, or doing what they can to achieve trans-boundary objectives such as glo-bal environmental goals. A bond regime could at last stimulate people to tackle climate change and war with the same resolve and ingenuity that cur-rently support many millions at unprecedented levels of health and prosperity.

Better solutions to local, national and global problems—that is the promise of Social Policy Bonds. But at the individual level, the benefits of efficient, effec-tive solutions would be profound. People would enjoy a better physical and social environment.

We do not know whether a bond regime would mean a larger or smaller role for government—something that preoccupies many who ponder policy in governments, think-tanks, or the academic world. More efficient government could mean lower taxes but on the other hand people, seeing that their taxes were generating better outcomes more efficiently, might vote for parties that promise greater public spending.

Resources are always going to be limited and Social Policy Bonds would not change that. Priorities and choices will always have to be made: under the Social Policy Bond principle, governments would still decide on which prob-lems to solve, and on the sums allocated to their solution. But democratic gov-ernments are good at representing and articulating their people's wishes. Where they are not so successful is in working out the most efficient ways of achieving these goals. This achievement is really a matter of allocating scarce resources. In economic theory, and on all the evidence, markets are the best way of allocating scarce resources to achieve prescribed ends. Social Policy Bonds would allow both government and the market to do what each is best at doing: respectively: prescribing ends, and allocating resources to meet these ends.

Government-backed Social Policy Bonds targeting global poverty, malnutri-tion or deadly conflicts are most probably a long way into the future. Before they become an accepted instrument of government policy, Social Policy Bonds will probably have to be issued on a smaller scale, gradually refined, and become widely and successfully deployed at the national level. But there is nothing to stop groups of private individuals issuing their own Social Policy Bonds, perhaps as complements to existing efforts of governments and NGOs—and that is the subject of this book's Annex.

For government to relinquish most of its discretion as to how to achieve social and environmental goals would require some courage as well as humility.[1] Yet in doing so, a government would not be renouncing its existing sanctions against illegal acts. It would still be deciding on the social and environmental outcomes that it wishes to target, and it would still be the ultimate source of finance for achieving them. In fact, the current system, when viewed impartially, would appear to be far more irrational. Under it, large proportions of national income are spent in pursuit of nebulous goals, few of which are costed, some of which conflict with each other, and many of which primarily benefit the better off—some of them already very wealthy indeed. Administering this expenditure is a burgeoning bureaucracy, which, on the rare occasions its performance is even measured, is usually shown to be inefficient, if not completely useless. So it is that with a massive public sector, and after decades of high and rising taxation, the Government of the United Kingdom, the world's fourth wealthiest economy, is still targeting the birth weight of babies in the country's most disadvantaged areas.[138]

---

1. There is a fascinating parallel here with the individual psyche. Our thinking can be analytic or intuitive. The analytic is useful in problem-solving, where assessment acts on selective information stored in memory to generate solutions. This corresponds to policymaking that uses existing activities or institutions to achieve a goal. Intuitive thinking is ideal for situations that do not lend themselves to specific analysis, such as choice of marriage partner, or how to plan one's work life. This corresponds to letting markets find out how a goal shall be achieved, rather than specifying a particular approach. 'Unfortunately, as people grow up and are increasingly schooled in analytic thinking, they move further and further from trusting their intuition. This leads to unbalanced, overused and ultimately abused analytic thinking in which people over-think issues that are more appropriate to creative resolution using the other mode.' Policymakers tend to follow the same pattern: prescribing that problems shall be addressed by a limited range of pre-used, uncontroversial policies, rather than trusting people to come up with innovative and efficient solutions. (For a summary of the two sorts of thinking and for the source of the quote, see, *A strength-based practice model: psychology of mind and health realization*, Stephen G. Wartel, 'Families in Society: The Journal of Contemporary Human Services', Alliance for Children and Families, 2003. The parallel is this author's.)

The acceptance of a Social Policy Bond regime, even with the aim of achieving national goals as uncontroversial as lower crime rates, or better health and education outcomes, may be politically difficult, and must be a gradual process. But the potential benefits should not be ignored. By injecting market forces into the achievement of social and environmental goals, Social Policy Bonds could achieve these goals more cost-effectively. And by enlarging the pool of potential problem-solvers they could make feasible, for the first time, such seemingly unattainable goals as world peace.

Annex:
Issuing your own Social Policy Bonds—a guide for social entrepreneurs

Why issue your own bonds?

As a private individual, or as a member of a group of concerned private individuals, you could issue and back your own Social Policy Bonds. You might feel particularly strongly about a local, national or even a global problem that is currently being ignored or dealt with inadequately. You might be especially frustrated by problems in the developing countries that you believe could be solved by circumventing, co-opting or undermining the corrupt, failing governments that stand in the way. That some developing country governments do not always have the welfare of their citizens at heart is, unfortunately, easy to show. Take this story about Nigeria, for instance:

> An outbreak of polio has hit children in the Nigerian state of Kano. Kano is one of the Muslim states that had boycotted the use of the polio vaccine. Many Muslim states in Nigeria banned the polio vaccine because those in charge said the Americans were using the vaccines to make their population infertile..... Despite appeals from neighbouring countries to vaccinate its population, the conspiracy theorists in Nigeria got their way. Now, as expected, polio is beginning to spread among children in the region.[139]

In such instances, a frankly mercenary approach—bribing the state authorities to take a long golfing holiday, for example—might be preferable to trying to

142

work with them. More generally, any Social Policy Bonds you issue could complement the measures that more enlightened governments, voluntary agencies and non-governmental organisations (NGOs) are undertaking.

Why not just give your millions to charity instead? Charities do marvellous work with limited resources, but there are things that they cannot do, no matter how dedicated. This especially applies in the developing countries. Charitable bodies cannot readily use their funds to bribe officials either to do their job properly or to look the other way when necessary. They cannot deliberately undermine those in power who are opposed to their cause and determined to resist it. They cannot, in short, play hardball even when doing so would greatly benefit thousands of innocent people. It is not just a matter of standing up to the thugs, kleptocrats, ideologues, politicians, generals, and the men of religion who do so much to keep their subject peoples poor and ignorant. It is also a matter of bringing financial self-interest—greed, in other words—into the equation. Social Policy Bonds would inject market forces into the achievement of goals that currently depend almost entirely on people's goodwill.

Markets are the most efficient means yet discovered of allocating society's scarce resources. They have had a bad press because most people associate them with capitalism red in tooth and claw, with extremes of wealth and poverty, or with raping the environment. But there is nothing inherently evil about markets. Concerned individuals or organisations can use them to serve public, as well as private, goals; Social Policy Bonds could channel the market's efficiencies and incentives into the achievement of such goals.

Let us assume that your particular goal is to raise female literacy in Pakistan, currently about 36 per cent.[140] You issue Female Literacy Bonds, because you believe female literacy is both an end in itself, and a means to other ends. Once your bonds have been auctioned to the highest bidders, bondholders would have incentives to carry out a wider range of literacy-raising initiatives than either governments or NGOs, and to do so more cost-effectively. Apart from bypassing or buying off the people in authority who block progress toward higher literacy rates, bondholders could lobby the Pakistani Government to give a higher priority to literacy in schools, or they could develop literacy-teaching projects of their own. They might finance the production of literacy programmes for TV, or set up village schools, or give prizes to the most literate families in villages. It would be up to bondholders to decide on those projects that will give them the highest increase in female literacy per unit outlay. The market prices of the bonds, and their changes over time, will generate helpful information as to how fast the objective is being achieved (see Chapter 6). These prices would be publicly quoted, just like those of ordinary bonds or shares. The literacy of random samples of 14-year old Pakistani girls could be measured annually by pre-selected reading tests. Once the 95 per cent target had been reached and sustained for, say, three years, you would redeem the bonds.

Some in the Pakistani Government, religious institutions or militant organisations might resent the targeting of such objectives by external agencies in this way. But while under the current system they can oppose literacy teaching in ways that attract support, under a Social Policy Bond regime they would have openly to declare their opposition to female literacy itself. It is precisely this focus on your desired *outcome*—rather than activities or institutions—that would strengthen the coalition working to achieve it.

Defining the redemption terms

You should take some care in defining the terms under which the bonds you issue shall be redeemed. The bonds would work by generating financial incentives for people to achieve particular goals. Unfortunately some people might try to fulfil the objective by complying with the letter of your redemption terms, rather than the spirit. If you issue Social Policy Bonds targeting the literacy rate of girls and young women in Pakistan you would be unwise to rely on the Pakistani Government's literacy tests. That Government or its agents could succumb to pressure from unscrupulous bondholders to falsify the results of any reading tests that would determine whether a literacy objective had been reached or not. The solution? You would stipulate, as a condition for redeeming the bonds, that any reading tests would be undertaken by an impartial body. You might be able to identify a trustworthy agency already carrying out robust literacy tests that, with a little customising, could fit your criteria. You must, of course, be certain that its test results will be an accurate indicator of female literacy in Pakistan.

One potential pitfall is that your bonds might induce people to modify their behaviour in ways that, while not illegal, would undermine what you were trying to achieve. For example, holders of Female Literacy Bonds might decide that the most effective way of raising female literacy would be to persuade all schoolteachers in Pakistan to drop the teaching of, say, arithmetic, to females and spend all their time on reading programmes instead. You might think this would be a worthwhile trade-off, but what if bondholders instead convinced charities to stop distributing food aid, or family planning supplies, in order to concentrate on teaching literacy? You could anticipate this by incorporating provisos into the bonds' redemption conditions. For example, you could stipulate that bonds shall not be redeemed if real spending on other teaching projects fell below 100 per cent of the levels prevailing when the bonds are issued.

If you target higher levels of literacy, some bondholders may be tempted to lobby in favour of easier reading tests. Again by judicious specification of the targeted objective you could forestall the problem: the bonds could stipulate the exact reading test to be used, or that the test would have to be certified as appropriate by a specified panel of impartial literacy experts.

Social Policy Bonds and government

Government has the power to pass laws that would affect bond prices, or its actions could influence bond prices in other ways. The Pakistani Government, for example, could come under great pressure from holders of bonds targeting female literacy to increase its spending on literacy programmes. Bondholders would lobby for such changes and they would obviously benefit financially if they were successful. But this would be no bad thing: the source of the pressure, and the motivation for it, would be easy to identify, and anyway lobbying is a legitimate activity. There is no reason why bondholders, in common with other pressure groups, should not lobby politicians. They might of course be doing so mainly out of financial self-interest. But existing pressure groups are also self-interested and, provided your objective is responsibly chosen, bondholders' self-interest will be channelled into valuable social benefit.

Lobbying, of course, already goes on because governments are always making decisions that create winners and losers. People become wealthy by exerting influence on politicians under the current system, but they and their effects on behaviour are not always identifiable. As now, under a Social Policy Bond regime it would be up to politicians to weigh the evidence for and against any course of action promoted by lobbyists, with due regard to the lobbyists' motivation. The sources of this sort of pressure, and the motivation for it, would be more transparent than under the current system so bondholders' lobbying need not pose any significant problems.

When they assess the value of the bonds, potential investors would take into account possible changes in legislation and their potential influence on the speed at which the targeted objective could be achieved. And it would be up to potential investors in Social Policy Bonds to take into account likely or possible changes in the legislative environment when bidding for the bonds.

There would be, and need be, nothing to prevent government agencies, as competitive suppliers of objective-achieving services, from buying any bonds that you issue, and participating as any other investors in the bonds.

You should check the legal status of Social Policy Bonds before you issue (or purchase) them. Some US states, for example, might see the bonds as lottery tickets, and their redemption as a lottery prize. This could affect their viability.[141]

Social Policy Bonds and existing institutions

Few bodies charged with achieving social goals are currently paid in ways that encourage better performance. Nevertheless some charities or NGOs are the main sources of expertise for solving social problems and some of them are bound to be cost-effective. How would your issuing Social Policy Bonds bear on their operations? The decision would be up to bondholders. They might investigate the activities of these bodies and help to finance those that were most cost-effective. Or they might find it more efficient to set up their own bodies devoted to achieving the objective that you are targeting.

If your bonds represented a large potential source of funds, existing organisations might themselves react by reviewing the results of their programmes and projects. They would focus their attention on the cost-effectiveness of their operations. If they could convince bondholders of their efficiency they would stand a greater chance of receiving more funding from them.

What happens once your objective has been achieved?

Once your objective is close to being achieved, you could float a new set of Social Policy Bonds aimed at maintaining the achieved outcome or at further improvements. Sustaining the outcome beyond the period specified in the original bond issue would probably be cheaper than achieving it in the first place, while further improvements targeted by a second bond issue would most likely cost less, in terms of benefit per unit outlay, than those achieved by the first issue (see Chapter 7).

Some practical aspects

Generating interest

One way to proceed might be to gather 'seed capital' from a group of wealthy, like-minded individuals. You could deposit these funds into an escrow account, to be used to redeem the bonds that you issue. You could then solicit donations from members of the public, who could deposit funds into this account, swelling the redemption fund. When a bond fund increases over time in this way, you could each bond's redemption value constant and issue more bonds, or you could stipulate that each bond would be redeemed for a fixed proportion of whatever will be the total value of the fund at the time of redemption.

Trading

Transactions costs tend to be low for financial instruments, but set-up costs, especially for initial issues of Social Policy Bonds might be fairly high. Remember, though, that allocation of funds under a bond regime would not take time and energy away from donors or charity administrators: that would be done by bondholders. Prospective investors in bonds might use web-based trading platforms: see the list of web-sites at the end of this Annex. Funds in the escrow account would earn interest until the bonds are redeemed.

Social Policy Bonds for all

- If you are cash-rich but time-poor and know what you want, then you could get together with like-minded people, set up an escrow account and issue your own bonds. If you are less wealthy you could seek out other like-minded individuals and pool your resources.

- If you are even less wealthy you could contribute to the funds set up by wealthy individuals, augmenting their bond redemption funds by depositing your spare cash into the escrow accounts they set up.

- If you have more energy than money you could buy Social Policy Bonds issued by someone else and then work to achieve the targeted objective. Your bonds would appreciate in value as the objective came closer to achievement. You could even borrow on the strength of the expected increase in capital value of your bonds, in order to finance objective-targeting projects. You could co-operate with other bond-holders in financing those activities that you think will be most efficient in achieving the target.

- If you are cash-poor but already helping to achieve a goal such as raising literacy in a developing country you could contact holders of Social Policy Bonds targeting literacy and if they believe your activities are efficient in reducing conflict they will find it worthwhile to help finance your existing projects.

Raising literacy of women in Pakistan is one objective suitable for targeting by philanthropists: it is worthwhile in its own right, it is measurable, and it requires diverse, responsive approaches that more suited to a Social Policy Bond regime than a top-down, one-size-fits-all policy. Are there other objectives amenable to targeting by privately backed bond issues? Apart from local environmental objectives, such as the air or water quality of particular cities, rivers or lakes, a strong contender could be nuclear peace: bondholders could issue bonds that are redeemable after, say, 30 years if there is no nuclear explosion, anywhere in the world, that kills more than a low, specified, number of 100 civilians.

Internet sites of interest to prospective bond issuers

One starting point would be the links in the 'New Trading Platforms' section on this page from Professor Robert Shiller's web-site: http://newfinancialorder.com/weblinks.htm

An alternative is the American Action Market at: http://www.americanactionmarket.org/concept.htm

Another possibility is using free web-based software, written to allow community currency groups to add an internet dimension to their LETS, HOURS, or Time Dollar systems. See: http://www.hughbarnard.org/cgi-bin/weblets/webtool.cgi

Epilogue

The Social Policy Bond concept has had an unusual fate for an unusual idea. It has been in the public domain for about 15 years, and it has not been so far been adopted anywhere, to my knowledge. But neither has it been dismissed outright. It tends to provoke initial enthusiasm amongst economists and decision makers, but then to be forgotten as day-to-day issues demand immediate attention. Robert Shiller, Professor of Economics at Yale University, wrote to me at the end of 1996, praising the Social Policy Bond idea, saying that it creates 'a large interest group for the solution of important problems. The political and other effects of creating such an interest group could be incalculable.' An earlier draft of this book elicited extreme comments at both ends of the range from the two referees: one dismissed the text as an irrelevance. The other called the idea 'original and ingenious' and 'a substantial contribution to debate about public policy'.

The Social Policy Bond concept is perhaps a difficult one for people to grasp. It does not fit neatly into any ideological box. In channelling market forces into the achievement of social and environmental goals, it can be seen simplistically, as a 'right-wing' way of achieving 'left-wing' objectives. Unfortunately, rather than appealing to both sets of ideologues it seems to appeal to neither!

In April 2002, I presented a paper on the bond concept to joint meeting of the Agriculture and Environment Committees at the Organisation for Economic Cooperation and Development (OECD) in Paris. At the meeting delegations from most of the OECD's member countries made comments on the paper. These were mostly along the lines of 'this is very interesting—but unworkable in practice.' Perhaps one of the delegates articulated the deeper feelings of those present, who were overwhelmingly government employees: 'if this gets adopted we'll all be out of jobs!' My OECD paper went no further.

I am pleased though that, at the time of writing, certain private individuals have taken the initiative and are proposing to issue their own Social Policy Bonds. They are considering floating bonds for projects as diverse as boosting voter registration, raising literacy in developing countries and developing open-source software. Enthused by the bond concept, they are raising funds, or preparing to put up their own funds, to redeem bonds targeting objectives that they specify. I am heartened and encouraged by their efforts.

Bibliography

Investing for the future, Ronnie Horesh, UK CEED Bulletin No 35, Centre for Economic and Environmental Development, Cambridge, UK, September-October 1991. (Presented as Room Document 3 to the December 1994 meeting of the OECD Joint Working Party of the Committee for Agriculture and the Environment Policy Committee.)

Social Policy Bonds: Injecting market incentives into the solution of social problems), Ronnie Horesh, AEU Occasional Papers, University of Cambridge, Cambridge, UK, August 1992.

Injecting incentives into the solution of social problems: Social Policy Bonds, Ronnie Horesh, Economic Affairs, **20** (3), Institute of Economic Affairs, London, September 2000.

Injecting incentives into the solution of social and environmental problems: Social Policy Bonds, Ronnie Horesh, iUniversity Press, Lincoln, Nebraska, USA. ISBN: 0-595-15374-7, January 2001.

Better than Kyoto: how Climate Stability Bonds can inject market incentives into the achievement of a stable climate, Ronnie Horesh, Writers Club Press, USA. ISBN: 0-595-21164-X, December 2001.

Better than Kyoto: Climate Stability Bonds, Ronnie Horesh, Economic Affairs, **22** (3), Institute of Economic Affairs, London, September 2002.

Market incentives to end war, Ronnie Horesh, Writers Club Press, USA, ISBN: 0-595-29484-7, September 2003.

Websites

http://SocialGoals.com *Social Policy Bonds*: the first three papers listed under 'Bibliography' can be downloaded free of charge from this site, which also contains links to online retailers of the book cited as the remaining bibliographic reference, and the email address of the author of this book.

http://users.rcn.com/wware1/spb-game.html *SPB the game*: online simulation of Social Policy Bonds.

http://www.openknowledge.org/writing/open-source/scb/ *The Wall Street Performer Protocol.* Using Software Completion Bonds to fund open source software development.

Endnote

[1] Almost half of adults have maths skills below those needed for the lowest possible GCSE pass grade, a government survey suggests. The Department for Education and Skills blamed "decades of neglect" for figures showing millions of people lacking basic literacy and numeracy skills. Source: BBC Online, 30 Oct 2003.

[2] "Indeed, richer nations not only fail to get happier as national income grows; even as their average level of happiness stays constant, the small fraction of the population suffering from serious psychopathology expands. More people become chronically depressed, and the suicide rate often rises." *Will Globalization Make You Happy?* Robert Wright, 'Foreign Policy', Fall 2000.

[3] *How not to buy happiness*, Robert H Frank, 'Daedalus', Spring 2004.

[4] "Once your nation attains a fairly comfortable standard of living, more income brings little, if any, additional happiness. In the United States between 1975 and 1995, real per capita GDP grew by 43 percent, but the average happiness of Americans didn't budge." Robert Wright, op cit, note 2.

[5] General government total outlays (current plus capital outlays) in 2004 are estimated at 40.3 per cent of nominal GDP for the OECD countries. Source: OECD.

[6] *SIPRI Yearbook 2004*, Stockholm International Peace Research Institute, June 2004. Figure is for the year 2003, and represents a rise of 18 per cent in real terms from the previous year.

[7] *Agricultural policies in OECD countries: monitoring and evaluation 2003*, OECD, Paris, 2003.

[8] *Distributional effects of agricultural support in selected OECD countries*, OECD, Paris, 1999.

[9] Ibid.

[10] *British watchdog criticises EU as fraud soars 75% to 700m*, P Waugh, 'The Independent', London, 30 May 2002.

[11] These figures come from *Perverse Incentives: Subsidies and Sustainable Development*, A P G de Moor, Institute for Research on Public Expenditure, The Netherlands,   1996:   http://www.worldpolicy.organisation/Americas/ environment/subsidies.html.

[12] *The strategy of equality: redistribution and the social services*, Julian Le Grand, George Allen and Unwin, London, 1982. The author points out that a major declared objective of government spending on social services has always been redistribution of wealth to the poor. But, after examining the impact of public expenditure on health, education, housing and transport in the UK, he concluded that in almost all the forms he scrutinised, it was distributed in favour of the higher social groups. Although the details of his results are obviously not up-to-date, the general features are still relevant.

[13] Just one example: "In 1999 a government-funded study by the [Japan] Housing Loan Administration Corp. found that of 116 construction-related loans it examined in detail, 42% involved organized crime." From *The Yakuza Recession*, 'Far Eastern Economic Review', 17 January 2002.

[14] A P G de Moor, op cit, note 11.

[14.5] *Escaping the subsidy trap*, Saferworld, Oxford, UK, ISBN: 1-904833-05-5 22 September 2004.

[15] *The end of history and the last man*, Francis Fukuyama, USA, 1992.

[16] *Lords of Poverty: The Power, Prestige, and Corruption of the International Aid Business*, Graham Hancock, 1989.

[17] Global Warming Information Center, National Center for Public Policy Research, Washington DC, www.nationalcenter.org.

[18] *The Truth about the Environment*, Bjorn Lomborg, 'The Economist', 4 August 2001.

[19] *Harbingers of doom*, Fred Pearce, 'New Scientist', 24 July 2004.

[20] *The darkening Earth: less sun at the Earth's surface complicates climate models*, David Appell, 'Scientific American', 2 August 2004.

[21] *Beach bugs make for a cooler world*, Peter Hadfield, 'New Scientist', 12 July 1997 (page 17).

[22] Saferworld, UK http://saferworld.org.uk.

[23] Saferworld, UK http://saferworld.org.uk; estimate by the United Nations High Commissioner for Refugees.

[24] Saferworld, UK http://saferworld.org.uk.

[25] *The horror of land mines*, Gino Strada, 'Scientific American', May 1996 (pages 40–45).

[26] *Peoples versus states*, Ted Robert Gurr, United States Institute of Peace Press (chapter 2), 2000.

[27] *World refugee survey*, published annually by the United States Committee for Refugees.

[28] *Peace and conflict 2001: a global survey of armed conflicts, self-determination movements, and democracy* Gurr T R, Marshall M G, Khosla, D, Center for International Development and Conflict Management, University of Maryland, 2001.

[29] Ibid.

[30] *Global conflict trends*, http://members.aol.com/CSPmgm/conflict.htm webpage maintained by Center for Systemic Peace, Policy IV project, dated 20 September 2000, sighted 21 August 2003.

[31] *Peoples versus states 2001*, op cit note 26 (chapter 6).

[32] *Peace and conflict 2001*, op cit note 28.

[33] *Global conflict trends,* op cit note 30.

[34] *The horror of land mines,* Gino Strada, 'Scientific American', May 1996 (pages 40–45).

[35] *SIPRI Yearbook 2002,* Stockholm International Peace Research Institute, June 2002.

[36] See *An American Hiroshima,* by Nicholas D Kristof, 'New York Times', 11 August 2004. Mr Kristof is reporting the views of Professor Graham Allison, of Harvard University, author of *Nuclear Terrorism,* Times Books, August 2004.

[37] "The conviction that any one group has exclusive possession of truth and goodness is a root cause of prejudice and boundaries that allow for discrimination and worse." *War Cries,* Oliver McTernan, 'The Times', 12 August 2003.

[38] *From reaction to conflict prevention,* Fen Osler Hampson and David M. Malone, editors, Boulder: Lynne Rienner, 2002.

[39] *The cycle of violence,* Cathy Widom, 'Science', vol 244, 1989 (pages 160–66).

[40] *The global menace of local strife,* 'The Economist', 24 May 2003 (page 26).

[41] *The economics of war: the intersection of need, creed and greed,* Conference Report, Woodrow Wilson International Center for Scholars, Washington, D.C. 10 September, 2001.

[42] Elizabeth Picard of the Institut de Recherche et d'Etudes sur le Monde Arabe et Méditerranéan, speaking at: *The economics of war: the intersection of need, creed and greed,* Conference Report, Woodrow Wilson International Center for Scholars, Washington, D.C. 10 September, 2001.

[43] *Statistics of deadly quarrels,* Richardson, Lewis F. Edited by Quincy Wright and C. C. Lienau. Pittsburgh: Boxwood Press, 1960.

[44] Ibid.

[45] Ibid.

[46] *War and peace*, Leo Tolstoy (translated by Ann Dunnigan), New York: Signet Classic, 1968 (page 730).

[47] Much of this section originates in *Post-Cold War opportunity and challenge*, 'Conflict prevention: a guide', Conflict Prevention Web, Creative Associates International.

[48] Ibid.

[49] *Violent conflicts 1400 A.D. to the present in different regions of the world*, Peter Brecke, Sam Nunn School of International Affairs, Georgia Institute of Technology, Atlanta, United States. Paper prepared for the 1999 Meeting of the Peace Science Society (International) on 8–10 October 1999 in Ann Arbor, Michigan, United States.

[50] *SIPRI Yearbook 2002*, Stockholm International Peace Research Institute, June 2002.

[51] *Post-Cold War Opportunity and Challenge*, op cit note 47.

[52] Ibid.

[53] *Economic growth, civil wars, and spatial spillovers*, Murdoch, James C. and Sandler T., Paper prepared for the Conference on 'Data Collection on Armed Conflict', Uppsala, Sweden, 8–9 June 2001.

[54] *2001 Report: Criteria to authorise or refuse arms exports*, Romeva, R. Paper prepared for the Conference on 'Data Collection on Armed Conflict', Uppsala, 8–9 June 2001.

[55] *Privatising peacemaking*, Doug Brooks, Bradlow Fellow, South Africa Institute of International Affairs, in conversation with Stephen Mbogo of 'West Africa', 18 September 2000.

[56] Ibid.

[57] Stockholm International Peace Research Institute, op cit, note 6.

[58] *The Military Balance 2000/2001*, International Institute for Strategic Studies, October 2000.

[59] *United Nations peacekeeping: Questions and answers.* http://www.un. organisation/Depts/dpko/dpko/ques.htm, sighted 22 May 2003.

[60] *Security with a human face: a proposal to create a Human Security Report*, web page prepared by Andy Mack following 'Euroconference' on 'Identifying Wars: Systematic Conflict Research and its Utility in Conflict Prevention and Resolution', Uppsala, Sweden, 8–9 June 2001.

[61] *Assessing the societal and systemic impact of warfare*, Monty G. Marshall, in, 'From Reaction to Prevention: Opportunities for the UN System in the New Millennium', edited by David Malone and Fen Osler Hampson, International Peace Academy. Lynne Rienner Publishers, 2001.

[62] See *Alternative endings,*' Radio Times', 13 July 2002. This was the subject of a (UK) Channel 4 documentary *Death: you're better off with cancer,* broadcast on 16 July 2002.

[63] *The WHO must drop old-style politics and get back to saving children's lives*, Roger Bate, 'Daily Telegraph', 10 May 2004.

[64] Basic Skills Agency report, May 2000.

[64.5] *Red sky at morning: America and the crisis of the global environment*, James Gustave Speth, Yale University Press, 2004.

[65] See *Happiness is a warm vote*, 'The Economist', 17 April 1999.

[66] "The point where more wealth ceases to imply more happiness is around $10,000 per capita annually", says Robert Wright, summarising work in this area in *Will globalization make you happy?*, op cit note 2.

[67] *Too many students*, Alison Wolf, 'Prospect', July 2002.

[68] BBC News Online, 2 December, 1999.

[69] International Adult Literacy Survey, 1998, (the figure of eight million applies to Britain). This Survey also says that while in Britain over 20 per cent of the population falls into the low skills category; in Europe the figure is around 10 per cent.

[70] *Green minister pushes for farming reform: One in five farms will be organic in 10 years' time if the government's policy goes according to plan*, Bettina Wassener, 'Financial Times', London, 12 June 2001.

[71] See, for instance, *Urban myths of organic farming*, Anthony Trewavas, 'Nature' **410**, 22 March 2001.

[72] *Paper versus polystyrene: a complex choice*, Martin B Hocking, 'Science' **251**, pp 504–5, 1 February 1991.

[73] *Energy and environmental profile analysis of children's disposable and cloth diapers*, Franklin Associates Ltd, Prairie Village, KS, USA, July 1990.

[74] For example, in Chester, UK: see 'Chester Standard', June 2002, and *Waste of time*, 'The Economist', 6 July 2002 (page 48), about recycling in New York.

[75] *The spirit of reform: managing the New Zealand state sector in a time of change*, Allen Schick, State Services Commission, Wellington, 1996.

[76] *Looping the Loop: Evaluating Outcomes and other risky feats* and *Essential Ingredients: Improving the quality of policy advice*, [New Zealand] State Services Commission, 1999 (www.ssc.govt.nz).

[77] *The spirit of reform*, op cit note 75

[78] *Guide to Assessing Agency Annual Performance Plans*, General Accounting Office of the USA (1997), (www.gao.gov/special.pubs).

[79] *Results Oriented Government: GPRA has established a solid foundation for achieving greater results*, GAO-04-38, US General Accounting Office, March 2004, www.gao.gov/cgi-bin/getrpt?GAO-04-38.

[80] Ibid, page 12.

[81] Ibid, page 7.

[82] Ibid, highlights page.

[83] Ibid, page 9.

[84] *Healthy people: the Surgeon General's Report on Health Promotion and Disease Prevention*, Public Health Service, US Department of Health, Education and Welfare, 1979. Publication No PHS 79-55071.

[85] *Promoting Health/Preventing Disease: Objectives for the Nation*. Washington, D.C., U.S. Dept. of Health and Human Services, 1980.

[86] *Healthy People 2000: National Health Promotion and Disease Prevention Objectives*, US Department of Health and Human Services, Publication No PHS 91-50212, 1990.

[87] *Objectives-Setting for Improved Health: The Public Health Service Healthy People Program*

[88] Ibid, page 4.

[89] *Results Oriented Government*, op cit note 79, page 13.

[90] Ibid, pages 16, 17 and 8, respectively.

[91] Ibid, page 14.

[92] Ibid, page 17.

[93] Ibid, page 17.

[94] Ibid, page 18.

[95] Ibid, page 19.

[96] *Why states believe foolish ideas: non-self-evaluation by states and societies*, Stephen Van Evera, MIT Political Science Department and Securities Studies Program, 10 January 2002, version 3.5.

[97] *Therapy culture*, Frank Furedi, Routledge, 2004 (Chapter 3, pp 60–61).

[98] *Democracy disconnected from the* electorate, Ralph Dahrendorf, Project Syndicate, 2004.

[99] John Kay, 'Financial Times', 8 May 2003.

[100] *Why states believe foolish ideas*, op cit note 96.

101 *A new public sector,* John Kay, 'Prospect', June 2001.

102 *The great granny grab,* Ross Clark, 'The Spectator', London, 17 August 2002.

103 *Country File,* BBC1 television, UK, 8 February 1998.

104 See Hayek, F A, 'The Pretence of Knowledge', in his *New Studies in Philosophy, Politics, Economics and the History of Ideas,* University of Chicago Press, Chicago, 1978.

105 Excerpts are from Article 39.

106 See, for example, *Happiness is a warm vote,* The Economist, 17 April 1999.

107 Kaiser/Harvard Program on the Public and Health/Social Policy Survey, January 1995. (From *On the contradictions of the people,* 'Marginal Revolution', 28 July 2004, http://www.marginalrevolution.com/marginalrevolution/2004/07/on_the_contradi, by Bryan Caplan.)

108 *The Skeptical Environmentalist: measuring the real state of the world,* Bjorn Lomborg, page 32

109 *The Skeptical Environmentalist: measuring the real state of the world,* Bjorn Lomborg, page 169

110 This discussion of Lomborg's failure to attribute environmental benefits to regulation originates in *Some realism about environmental skepticism,* Douglas A. Kysar

111 *Environmental indicators for agriculture, volume 3: methods and results,* OECD Paris, France (page 278).

112 *Statistics of deadly quarrels,* Brian Hayes, 'Computing Science', January–February 2002.

113 See *The thinkable,* by Bill Keller, 'New York Times', 4 May 2003.

114 Ibid.

[115] *The nuclear axis of evil*, Michael Ledeen, nationalreviewonline (http://www. nationalreview.com), 2 May 2003.

[116] *Data issues in the study of conflict*, Paul Collier and Anke Hoeffler, Paper prepared for the Conference on 'Data Collection on Armed Conflict', Uppsala, Sweden, 8–9 June 2001.

[117] Ibid.

[118] *Getting to war: predicting international conflict with mass media indicators*, W. Ben Hunt, University of Michigan Press, 1997.

[119] See the Center for Systemic Peace web page: http://members.aol.com/cspmgm/warcode.htm.

[120] *Notes on developing a Human Security/Insecurity Index*, Peter Brecke, Sam Nunn School of International Affairs, Georgia Institute of Technology, United States, 28 May 2002.

[121] *Africa: the heart of the matter*, 'The Economist', 13 May 2000.

[122] *Why states believe foolish ideas*, op cit note 96.

[123] *The global menace of local strife*, 'The Economist', 24 May 2003 (page 25).

[124] *The Balance Sheet*, John Kay, 'Prospect', July 2002.

[125] Ibid.

[126] Dr Jonathan Michie, Lecturer at the Judge Institute of Management Studies, and a Fellow of Robinson College, Cambridge, UK, speaking at a seminar on *The Elusive Concept of Sovereignty*, held at the Finnish Institute in April 1996.

[127] Arthur Andersen and Enterprise LSE, *Value for money drivers in the Private Finance Initiative*, commissioned by (UK) Treasury Taskforce, 17 January 2000.

[128] Ibid.

[129] *Healthy people: the Surgeon General's Report on Health Promotion and Disease Prevention*, Public Health Service, US Department of Health, Education and Welfare, 1979. Publication No PHS 79-55071.

[130] *State-building: governance and world order in the 21st century*, Francis Fukuyama, Cornell University Press, May 2004.

[131] See *Happiness is a warm vote*, 'The Economist', 17 April 1999.

[132] See *Height and the high life*, by Timothy Leunig and Hans-Joachim Voth, in *The economic future in historical perspective* by Paul A. David and Mark Price Thomas (editors), http://www.eh.net/bookreviews/library/0801.shtml.

[133] *Not just for the money: an economic theory of personal motivation*, Bruno S Frey, Edward Elgar, 1997.

[134] *Crowding out virtue*, Gerald F Gaus, Agenda, 5 (4), Australian National University, 1998. This is a short review of Bruno Frey's book, cited above (note 124).

[135] Ibid.

[136] *Japan, Refutation of Neoliberalism*, Robert Locke, 'Post-autistic economics review', issue no. 23, 5 January 2004, article 1, http://www.btinternet.com/pae_news/review/issue23.htm

[137] From *On the contradictions of the people*, 'Marginal Revolution', 28 July 2004, http://www.marginalrevolution.com/marginalrevolution/2004/07/on_the_contradi, by Bryan Caplan.

[138] See *Opportunity for All* (Chapter 2), the Poverty and Social Exclusion Team, Department of Social Security, London, September 1999.

[139] See http://www.medicalnewstoday.com/medicalnews.php?newsid=10275

[140] *Pakistan: Gap widens in male, female literacy rate*, 'ACR [Asia Child Rights] Weekly Newsletter', Vol 2, No 31, 30 July, 2003, Asian Human Rights Commission. The article reports figures from the recently published 'Pakistan Education and School Atlas', which shows the female literacy rate to have risen

from 16 per cent in 1980 to 33 per cent in 1997. The current rate of 36 per cent compares with a male literacy rate of 60 per cent.

[141] See http://www.arentfox.com/post/forum/csmessages/427.html.

0-595-33961-1